THE HISTORY & CULTURE of NATIVE AMERICANS

The Seminole

THE HISTORY & CULTURE of NATIVE AMERICANS

THE HISTORY & CULTURE of NATIVE AMERICANS

The Seminole

ANDREW K. FRANK

Series Editor
PAUL C. ROSIER

CHELSEA HOUSE PUBLISHERS
An imprint of Infobase Publishing

For my children—Daniel, Noah, and Shayna—who bring me endless joy

The Seminole

Copyright © 2011 by Infobase Publishing

Chelsea House
An imprint of Infobase Publishing
132 West 31st Street
New York NY 10001

Library of Congress Cataloging-in-Publication Data

Frank, Andrew, 1970-
  The Seminole / Andrew Frank.
    p. cm. — (The history and culture of Native Americans)
  Includes bibliographical references and index.
  ISBN 978-1-60413-790-3 (hardcover)
  1. Seminole Indians—History—Juvenile literature.   I. Title.   II. Series.

  E99.S28F73 2011
  975.9004'973859—dc22   2010017295

Chelsea House books are available at special discounts when purchased in bulk quantities
for businesses, associations, institutions, or sales promotions. Please call our Special Sales
Department in New York at (212) 967-8800 or (800) 322-8755.

You can find Chelsea House on the World Wide Web at
http://www.chelseahouse.com

Text design by Lina Farinella
Cover design by Alicia Post
Composition by Newgen
Cover printed by Bang Printing, Brainerd, Minn.
Book printed and bound by Bang Printing, Brainerd, Minn.
Date printed: October 2010
Printed in the United States of America

10 9 8 7 6 5 4 3 2 1
This book is printed on acid-free paper.

All links and Web addresses were checked and verified to be correct at the time of publication.
Because of the dynamic nature of the Web, some addresses and links may have changed since
publication and may no longer be valid.

Contents

Foreword
by Paul C. Rosier

Native American words, phrases, and tribal names are embedded in the very geography of the United States—in the names of creeks, rivers, lakes, cities, and states, including Alabama, Connecticut, Iowa, Kansas, Illinois, Missouri, Oklahoma, and many others. Yet Native Americans remain the most misunderstood ethnic group in the United States. This is a result of limited coverage of Native American history in middle schools, high schools, and colleges; poor coverage of contemporary Native American issues in the news media; and stereotypes created by Hollywood movies, sporting events, and TV shows.

Two newspaper articles about American Indians caught my eye in recent months. Paired together, they provide us with a good introduction to the experiences of American Indians today: first, how they are stereotyped and turned into commodities; and second, how they see themselves being a part of the United States and of the wider world. (Note: I use the terms *Native Americans* and *American Indians* interchangeably; both terms are considered appropriate.)

In the first article, "Humorous Souvenirs to Some, Offensive Stereotypes to Others," written by Carol Berry in *Indian Country Today,* I read that tourist shops in Colorado were selling "souvenir" T-shirts portraying American Indians as drunks. "My Indian name is Runs with Beer," read one T-shirt offered in Denver. According to the article, the T-shirts are "the kind of stereotype-reinforcing products also seen in nearby Boulder, Estes Park, and likely other Colorado communities, whether as part of the tourism trade or as everyday merchandise." No other ethnic group in the United States is stereotyped in such a public fashion. In addition, Native people are used to sell a range of consumer goods, including the Jeep Cherokee, Red Man chewing tobacco, Land O'Lakes butter, and other items that either objectify or insult them, such as cigar store Indians. As importantly, non-Indians learn about American Indian history and culture through sports teams such as the Atlanta Braves, Cleveland Indians, Florida State Seminoles, or Washington Redskins, whose name many American Indians consider a racist insult; dictionaries define *redskin* as a "disparaging" or "offensive" term for American Indians. When fans in Atlanta do their "tomahawk chant" at Braves baseball games, they perform two inappropriate and related acts: One, they perpetuate a stereotype of American Indians as violent; and two, they tell a historical narrative that covers up the violent ways that Georgians treated the Cherokee during the Removal period of the 1830s.

The second article, written by Melissa Pinion-Whitt of the San Bernardino *Sun* addressed an important but unknown dimension of Native American societies that runs counter to the irresponsible and violent image created by products and sporting events. The article, "San Manuels Donate $1.7 M for Aid to Haiti," described a Native American community that had sent aid to Haiti after it was devastated in January 2010 by an earthquake that killed more than 200,000 people, injured hundreds of thousands more, and destroyed the Haitian capital. The San Manuel Band of Mission Indians in California donated $1.7 million to help relief efforts in Haiti; San Manuel children held fund-raisers to collect additional donations. For the San Manuel Indians it was nothing new; in 2007 they had donated $1 million to help Sudanese refugees in Darfur. San Manuel also contributed $700,000 to relief efforts following Hurricane Katrina and Hurricane Rita, and donated $1 million in 2007 for wildfire recovery in Southern California.

Such generosity is consistent with many American Indian nations' cultural practices, such as the "give-away," in which wealthy tribal members give to the needy, and the "potlatch," a winter gift-giving ceremony and feast tradition shared by tribes in the

Pacific Northwest. And it is consistent with historical accounts of American Indians' generosity. For example, in 1847 Cherokee and Choctaw, who had recently survived their forced march on a "Trail of Tears" from their homelands in the American South to present-day Oklahoma, sent aid to Irish families after reading of the potato famine, which created a similar forced migration of Irish. A Cherokee newspaper editorial, quoted in Christine Kinealy's *The Great Irish Famine: Impact, Ideology, and Rebellion,* explained that the Cherokee "will be richly repaid by the consciousness of having done a good act, by the moral effect it will produce abroad." During and after World War II, nine Pueblo communities in New Mexico offered to donate food to the hungry in Europe, after Pueblo army veterans told stories of suffering they had witnessed while serving in the United States armed forces overseas. Considering themselves a part of the wider world, Native people have reached beyond their borders, despite their own material poverty, to help create a peaceful world community.

American Indian nations have demonstrated such generosity within the United States, especially in recent years. After the terrorist attacks of September 11, 2001, the Lakota Sioux in South Dakota offered police officers and emergency medical personnel to New York City to help with relief efforts; Indian nations across the country sent millions of dollars to help the victims of the attacks. As an editorial in the *Native American Times* newspaper explained on September 12, 2001, "American Indians love this country like no other. . . . Today, we are all New Yorkers."

Indeed, Native Americans have sacrificed their lives in defending the United States from its enemies in order to maintain their right to be both American and Indian. As the volumes in this series tell us, Native Americans patriotically served as soldiers (including as "code talkers") during World War I and World War II, as well as during the Korean War, the Vietnam War, and, after 9/11, the wars in Afghanistan and Iraq. Native soldiers, men and women, do so today by the tens of thousands because they believe in America, an

America that celebrates different cultures and peoples. Sgt. Leonard Gouge, a Muscogee Creek, explained it best in an article in *Cherokee News Path* in discussing his post-9/11 army service. He said he was willing to serve his country abroad because "by supporting the American way of life, I am preserving the Indian way of life."

This new Chelsea House series has two main goals. The first is to document the rich diversity of American Indian societies and the ways their cultural practices and traditions have evolved over time. The second goal is to provide the reader with coverage of the complex relationships that have developed between non-Indians and Indians over the past several hundred years. This history helps to explain why American Indians consider themselves both American and Indian and why they see preserving this identity as a strength of the American way of life, as evidence to the rest of the world that America is a champion of cultural diversity and religious freedom. By exploring Native Americans' cultural diversity and their contributions to the making of the United States, these volumes confront the stereotypes that paint all American Indians as the same and portray them as violent; as "drunks," as those Colorado T-shirts do; or as rich casino owners, as many news accounts do.

✳   ✳   ✳

Each of the 14 volumes in this series is written by a scholar who shares my conviction that young adult readers are both fascinated by Native American history and culture and have not been provided with sufficient material to properly understand the diverse nature of this complex history and culture. The authors themselves represent a varied group that includes university teachers and professional writers, men and women, and Native and non-Native. To tell these fascinating stories, this talented group of scholars has examined an incredible variety of sources, both the primary sources that historical actors have created and the secondary sources that historians and anthropologists have written to make sense of the past.

Although the 14 Indian nations (also called tribes and communities) selected for this series have different histories and cultures, they all share certain common experiences. In particular, they had to face an American empire that spread westward in the eighteenth and nineteenth centuries, causing great trauma and change for all Native people in the process. Because each volume documents American Indians' experiences dealing with powerful non-Indian institutions and ideas, I outline below the major periods and features of federal Indian policy-making in order to provide a frame of reference for complex processes of change with which American Indians had to contend. These periods—Assimilation, Indian New Deal, Termination, Red Power, and Self-determination—and specific acts of legislation that define them—in particular the General Allotment Act, the Indian Reorganization Act, and the Indian Self-determination and Education Assistance Act—will appear in all the volumes, especially in the latter chapters.

In 1851, the commissioner of the federal Bureau of Indian Affairs (BIA) outlined a three-part program for subduing American Indians militarily and assimilating them into the United States: concentration, domestication, and incorporation. In the first phase, the federal government waged war with the American Indian nations of the American West in order to "concentrate" them on reservations, away from expanding settlements of white Americans and immigrants. Some American Indian nations experienced terrible violence in resisting federal troops and state militia; others submitted peacefully and accepted life on a reservation. During this phase, roughly from the 1850s to the 1880s, the U.S. government signed hundreds of treaties with defeated American Indian nations. These treaties "reserved" to these American Indian nations specific territory as well as the use of natural resources. And they provided funding for the next phase of "domestication."

During the domestication phase, roughly the 1870s to the early 1900s, federal officials sought to remake American Indians in the mold of white Americans. Through the Civilization Program, which actually started with President Thomas Jefferson, federal officials sent religious missionaries, farm instructors, and teachers to the newly created reservations in an effort to "kill the Indian to save the man," to use a phrase of that time. The ultimate goal was to extinguish American Indian cultural traditions and turn American Indians into Christian yeoman farmers. The most important piece of legislation in this period was the General Allotment Act (or Dawes Act), which mandated that American Indian nations sell much of their territory to white farmers and use the proceeds to farm on what was left of their homelands. The program was a failure, for the most part, because white farmers got much of the best arable land in the process. Another important part of the domestication agenda was the federal boarding school program, which required all American Indian children to attend schools to further their rejection of Indian ways and the adoption of non-Indian ways. The goal of federal reformers, in sum, was to incorporate (or assimilate) American Indians into American society as individual citizens and not as groups with special traditions and religious practices.

During the 1930s some federal officials came to believe that American Indians deserved the right to practice their own religion and sustain their identity as Indians, arguing that such diversity made America stronger. During the Indian New Deal period of the 1930s, BIA commissioner John Collier devised the Indian Reorganization Act (IRA), which passed in 1934, to give American Indian nations more power, not less. Not all American Indians supported the IRA, but most did. They were eager to improve their reservations, which suffered from tremendous poverty that resulted in large measure from federal policies such as the General Allotment Act.

Some federal officials opposed the IRA, however, and pushed for the assimilation of American Indians in a movement called Termination. The two main goals of Termination advocates, during the 1950s and 1960s, were to end (terminate) the federal reservation system and American Indians' political sovereignty derived from treaties and to relocate American Indians from rural reservations to urban areas. These coercive federal assimilation policies in turn generated resistance from Native Americans, including young activists who helped to create the so-called Red Power era of the 1960s and 1970s, which coincided with the African-American civil rights movement. This resistance led to the federal government's rejection of Termination policies in 1970. And in 1975 the U.S. Congress passed the Indian Self-determination and Education Assistance Act, which made it the government's policy to support American Indians' right to determine the future of their communities. Congress then passed legislation to help American Indian nations to improve reservation life; these acts strengthened American Indians' religious freedom, political sovereignty, and economic opportunity.

All American Indians, especially those in the western United States, were affected in some way by the various federal policies described above. But it is important to highlight the fact that each American Indian community responded in different ways to these pressures for change, both the detribalization policies of assimilation and the retribalization policies of self-determination. There is no one group of "Indians." American Indians were and still are a very diverse group. Some embraced the assimilation programs of the federal government and rejected the old traditions; others refused to adopt non-Indian customs or did so selectively, on their own terms. Most American Indians, as I noted above, maintain a dual identity of American and Indian.

Today, there are more than 550 American Indian (and Alaska Natives) nations recognized by the federal government. They have a legal and political status similar to states, but they have special rights and privileges that are the result of congressional acts and the hundreds of treaties that still govern federal-Indian relations today. In July 2008, the total population of American Indians (and Alaska Natives) was 4.9 million, representing about 1.6 percent of the United States population. The state with the highest number of American Indians is California, followed by Oklahoma, home to the Cherokee (the largest American Indian nation in terms of population), and then Arizona, home to the Navajo (the second-largest American Indian nation). All told, roughly half of the American Indian population lives in urban areas; the other half lives on reservations and in other rural parts of the country. Like all their fellow American citizens, American Indians pay federal taxes, obey federal laws, and vote in federal, state, and local elections; they also participate in the democratic processes of their American Indian nations, electing judges, politicians, and other civic officials.

This series on the history and culture of Native Americans celebrates their diversity and differences as well as the ways they have strengthened the broader community of America. Ronnie Lupe, the chairman of the White Mountain Apache government in Arizona, once addressed questions from non-Indians as to "why Indians serve the United States with such distinction and honor?" Lupe, a Korean War veteran, answered those questions during the Gulf War of 1991–1992, in which Native American soldiers served to protect the independence of the Kuwaiti people. He explained in "Chairman's Corner" in *The Fort Apache Scout* that "our loyalty to the United States goes beyond our need to defend our home and reservation lands. . . . Only a few in this country really understand that the indigenous people are a national treasure. Our values have the potential of creating the social, environmental, and spiritual healing that could make this country truly great."

—Paul C. Rosier
Associate Professor of History
Villanova University

An Unconquered People

In December 2006, the Seminole Tribe of Florida bought the Hard Rock International. The tribe spent nearly $1 billion for this worldwide restaurant chain. The purchase surprised many. Decades earlier, the Seminole were poor, isolated, and largely unknown to outsiders. Now they were owners of an international corporation.

Seminole leaders knew that the purchase represented a new era in American Indian history. "Our ancestors sold Manhattan for trinkets," tribal council representative Max Osceola Jr. stated at a widely reported news conference on December 7, 2006. "Today with the acquisition of the Hard Rock Cafe, we're going to buy Manhattan back, one hamburger at a time." The message was clear. By owning the Hard Rock, the Florida Seminole would be in charge of a profitable global corporation. It was a visible reminder that American Indians were still alive and fighting for their communities. It also announced that the Seminole Tribe and other American Indian tribes could no longer be ignored.

Through the Hard Rock purchase, the Seminole became symbols of a new era of American Indian history. In this new era, American Indians would not always be victims of U.S. expansion. For centuries, this was not the case. American Indians were moved to make space for cotton fields and slavery. They were moved to make room for new cities. They were moved so other people could get access to natural resources such as oil, gold, and timber. Tribal concerns were considered to be less important than economic development. In the twenty-first century, tribal concerns are now driving forces in the U.S. economy.

THE SEMINOLE

The Seminole Tribe of Florida is widely known as the nation's only "unconquered" tribe. They formed two and a half centuries ago in northern Florida, largely as an offshoot of the Creek and other American Indian communities in Georgia and elsewhere. Since then, the Seminole have survived in spite of many obstacles. Its members are proud of the fact that they have never signed a peace treaty with the United States. They never surrendered.

The term *Seminole* has many translations. It seems to come from the Spanish term for runaway—*cimarron.* The term also translates to "wild people" or "fugitives"—terms that Europeans and then Americans widely used in order to ignore or degrade American Indian communities. Seminole and other Muskogee-speaking Native Americans have translated the term to be "those who camp at a distance."

The Seminole's reputation as an unconquered people is well earned. They began as survivors of the turmoil that followed the arrival of European explorers and settlers. For more than two centuries, they have followed paths of their own choosing.

The Seminole's unconquered status largely comes from their early history in the nineteenth century. The Florida Seminole

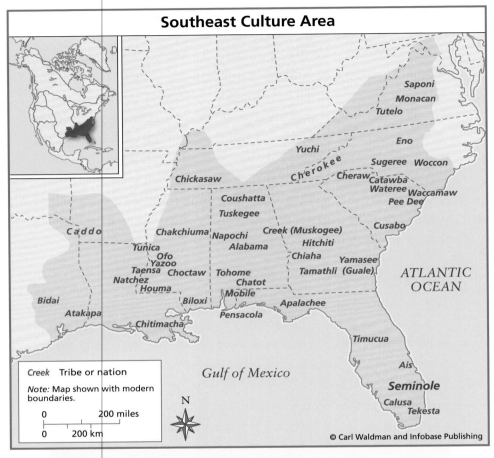

Southeast Culture Area

Major geographical features of the region in which the Southeast Indians lived included dense forest, coastal plains, subtropical swamps, floodplains, and mountains. Most Southeast Indians lived in river valleys. They were mainly farmers who also hunted, fished, and foraged.

fought three wars with the United States in the first half of the 1800s. The First Seminole War lasted from 1816 to 1818, the Second Seminole War lasted from 1835 to 1842, and the Third Seminole War lasted from 1855 to 1858. The United States spent more than $40 million fighting the Second Seminole War, a sum that was larger than all of the other U.S. wars up to that point. The United States also lost 1,700 soldiers during the second war. Despite a large investment of men and money, all of the wars ended in stalemates, or ties. The Seminole people were never defeated, and some Seminole warriors refused to lay down their arms.

Although greatly outnumbered and outgunned by the U.S. military, the Seminole successfully resisted all attempts to eliminate their presence in Florida. They suffered greatly in the process. Many Seminole were killed in the wars. Many more were forcibly removed to what was called Indian Territory, which is now the state of Oklahoma. Those who remained in Florida had to build new homes repeatedly. At the start of the first war, most Seminole lived in northern Florida. By the end of the third war, the Florida Seminole primarily lived in the southern part of the state.

The Seminole avoided being conquered through their bravery and hit-and-run military tactics. They and their families also took refuge in the wetlands and mangroves of Florida. The U.S. military was unwilling or unable to operate in these areas. At the end of each of the wars, the U.S. military withdrew from Florida and reluctantly allowed the surviving Seminole families to remain.

LIFE IN THE EVERGLADES

After the Third Seminole War ended in 1858, the Florida Seminole creatively found ways to survive in the varied but largely inhospitable environment of the Florida interior. This area was largely defined by Lake Okeechobee and the Everglades. Lake Okeechobee is the largest freshwater lake in Florida. The Everglades is widely known as the "river of grass." More precisely, it is subtropical wetlands. It contains freshwater ponds, prairies, sawgrass marshes, and forests. For centuries, it has been the home of a wide range of plants and animals. In the late 1800s, this ecosystem covered almost the entire southern part of the Florida peninsula.

In the late 1800s and early 1900s, the Seminole usually kept their distance from American settlers. During these years, the Seminole took advantage of the bounty of the Everglades. They traded animal pelts and hides as well as bird feathers with a few white settlers, but they survived primarily by hunting, fishing, gathering, and tending to small farms and gardens.

The Seminole are known for their unique cultural traditions, such as the number of beads worn by the Seminole women and their colorful patch-work garments (as seen on the girl above).

In their daily lives, they took advantage of and adjusted to the realities of life in and near the Everglades. They hunted new animals for their meat, hides, and feathers, which they sold. They turned alligator hides and egret plumes into commodities. They turned to new plants to gather, and they grew and harvested new crops.

In many ways, the Florida Seminole reshaped their daily lives to suit their new needs. They began to build a new style of home called chickees. These thatched-roof homes were ideally suited for the environment. The roofs were made primarily of palm fronds, which were widely available. They lacked exterior walls, allowing their inhabitants to enjoy a breeze in the often-sweltering heat of Florida. The floors were raised to provide protection from rain and flood waters, as well as from various animals. Although most Seminole do not live in chickees today, many have built these structures in their yards and communities for socializing and cooking.

The Seminole also created a new style of clothing called patchwork. American Indians of the Southeast have worn ornate and colorful clothing for centuries. The Seminole were no different. With the introduction of the sewing machine in the early twentieth century, Seminole women began to stitch together smaller pieces of cloth to make intricately designed garments. Certain designs and color patterns became synonymous with the Seminole.

Politically, the Florida Seminole eventually became leaders of a national campaign for tribal rights, and economically they have recently become successful global entrepreneurs. They have successfully waged legal battles in U.S. courts. Other tribes and other courts have looked to these legal victories for guidance.

TRIBAL RECOGNITION

Today, the Seminole Tribe of Florida is one of two federally recognized Seminole tribes. This means that it has a nation-to-nation relationship with the United States. A larger and lesser-known group of Seminole live in Oklahoma and are known as the Seminole Nation.

They are the other federally recognized Seminole group. The Oklahoma Seminole descend from Florida Seminole who were forcefully deported or forced to migrate west in the early nineteenth century.

Other Seminole live throughout the United States and elsewhere, often without tribal citizenship in either the Florida or Oklahoma nations. Some live integrated in other Native American or non-Native communities. Others are known as Independent Seminole. In addition to sharing their early history in Florida, these Seminole frequently share many of their cultural and religious beliefs. Over time, though, the Seminole of Florida and the Seminole of Oklahoma became two separate peoples and communities.

CULTURAL NORMS

Since their creation, the Florida Seminole have maintained several cultural and social traditions. Many of these traditions began among the American Indians who inhabited the Southeast many centuries ago. They are traditions that are shared by many of the other American Indian nations of the region: the Creek, Cherokee, Choctaw, and Chickasaw.

Seminole society is largely shaped by a system of clans, or extended families. These clans are normally named for things found in nature. Today the Seminole have eight clans: deer, snake, bear, otter, bird, big town, panther, and wind. Many centuries ago, there were several more.

Members of a clan consider themselves to be family, even if they cannot connect themselves on a family tree. Clans help determine how people associate with one another and participate in ceremonies. Clan membership gets passed down from mother to child. The clan of a father does not determine whose children are related to whom, or to which clan they belong.

Cultures that rely on the female line to trace kinship are called matrilineal. In matrilineal societies, networks of related women often form the backbone of a community. The Seminole are matrilineal, and like many other matrilineal communities, they typically build their homes near other maternal relatives. Members of clans also help raise each other's children and otherwise live interconnected lives.

The importance of Seminole women cannot be overstated. Traditionally, women provided most of the food that sustained Seminole individuals. Seminole women controlled the farm fields that typically contained corn, beans, and squash. Corn was widely considered a sacred item, and it served as the center of many rituals and beliefs. Women also were in charge of gathering nuts, berries, and other foods found in nature.

Whereas women controlled what happened inside a village, men controlled what happened between or outside of the villages. Seminole men were the hunters, traders, and diplomats. In other words, both women and men had power in the traditional Seminole world. The two kinds of roles complemented each other.

The Green Corn Ceremony, which is usually held in the late summer, is marked by dancing, feasting, fasting, and religious observations. This ceremony marks the Seminole New Year. Shown is a painting of the Corn Dance by the artist George Catlin.

Seminole individuals traditionally speak one of two languages: Mikasuki or Muskogee (Creek). In modern times, most Seminole also speak English. Historically, many Seminole spoke other Native American languages, as well as Spanish and French.

CEREMONIAL LIFE

The most important ceremony among the Seminole is the Green Corn Ceremony and the Corn Dance associated with it. American Indians throughout the Southeast have practiced a similar version of this ceremony for hundreds of years. The event lasts for several days and is held every spring.

The ceremony celebrates the harvest. The Seminole set up camps according to their clans and perform important dances and rituals. Many of these rituals deal with purifying individuals and the community. Other ceremonies are coming-of-age rituals or demonstrations of the manhood of participants. In addition, disputes between Seminole individuals are resolved during the event.

The Seminole have also passed down countless stories for generations. These stories help connect modern Native Americans with their ancestors. They also provide lessons that teach individuals how to behave and that explain the meanings of the natural world.

CONCLUSION

The Seminole are an interesting and resilient people. They have undergone one of the most remarkable transformations among Native American groups. They formed in the late 1700s, were devastated and divided by wars with the United States in the early 1800s, and struggled to survive for the next century. In the past two decades, however, the Seminole have enjoyed an economic and cultural revival. They are today a tribe that is deeply connected to their traditions and history even as they are very connected to the modern world.

Origins of
the Seminole

The Seminole are a modern entity, historically speaking. Although they do not have the equivalent of the Declaration of Independence or another founding document, historians think that they emerged as a distinct group in the eighteenth century. They are therefore roughly the same age as the United States. Just as the United States had a colonial history, the Seminole formed out of a complicated and interesting past. Their ancestors occupied Florida and the rest of the U.S. South for thousands of years and predated the arrival of the Spanish by centuries.

BEFORE THE SEMINOLE

When Spanish explorer Juan Ponce de León set the first European foot on Florida in 1513, the Seminole were not yet living there. In fact, they did not yet exist as a people. Instead, Florida contained

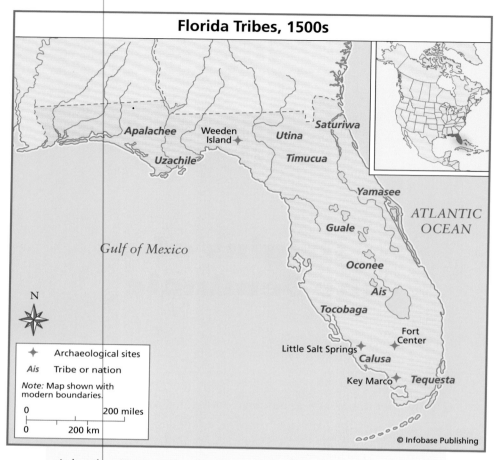

Florida Tribes, 1500s

Apalachee
Weeden Island
Utina
Saturiwa
Uzachile
Timucua
Yamasee
ATLANTIC OCEAN
Guale
Gulf of Mexico
Oconee
Ais
N
Tocobaga
Fort Center
Little Salt Springs
Calusa
Key Marco Tequesta

✦ Archaeological sites
Ais Tribe or nation
Note: Map shown with modern boundaries.

0   200 miles
0   200 km

© Infobase Publishing

In less than 200 years after the arrival of Ponce de León in 1513, most of the Native population had died due to wars with Europeans and newly introduced diseases to which the American Indians had no immunity. Historians do know that most of the northern Florida tribes were farmers and most of the southern Florida tribes depended on hunting and gathering.

several large Native American chiefdoms. The largest three chiefdoms were the Apalachee (in the panhandle), Timucua (in the northeast), and Calusa (in the southern and center of the territory). Scholars disagree over the total size of Florida's Native American population at the time, but most conclude that the area contained somewhere between 100,000 and 350,000 individuals.

On the eve of European contact, these American Indians lived in stable towns and villages and practiced mixed agriculture. They grew maize (corn), beans, squash, and other vegetables; they hunted deer, bear, rabbit, and other animals; and they gathered various root vegetables and berries that grew in the region. Communities located near the water frequently relied heavily on shellfish and various water animals for their dietary needs.

The American Indians of Florida also had specialized craftsmen and artists who made pottery and other valuable material and spiritual goods. They also built large earthen mounds throughout Florida and elsewhere. These were usually large circles or other geometric shapes, but they also were occasionally made in the shapes of animals. The mounds required a tremendous amount of labor and often took generations to build. They served various purposes: as burial grounds, to house ceremonial and political leaders, and as the center of residential communities.

Before the arrival of the Europeans, the Native Americans of Florida had rather complex political structures. They had strong chiefs who often obtained their positions as birthrights and expected obedience from followers. In these hierarchical communities, local villages paid tribute (or taxes) to chiefs in exchange for protection and as a sign of loyalty. These chiefdoms shared some general characteristics, but many differences separated them into competing identities. In addition to following different leaders, they also spoke different languages and had different religious beliefs and ceremonies.

THE ARRIVAL OF EUROPEANS

Juan Ponce de León was born in 1471 to a noble family of Spaniards from the village of Santervas de Campos in northern Spain. As an adult, Ponce de León fought in several campaigns against the Moors, and after some years he began looking for better opportunities. He found a great position sailing with Christopher Columbus on his second voyage, when the fleet reached the Caribbean in 1493. He later became frontier governor of a province called Higuey in Puerto Rico, where he married, had three daughters, and accumulated wealth. Still, rumors of undiscovered islands northwest of Hispaniola intrigued King Ferdinand of Spain, and Ponce de León was called on to set sail once again. On March 4, 1513, Ponce de León and at least 200 men set off from Puerto

Ponce de Leon wounded.

In 1513, Ponce de León arrived on the coast of Florida. European explorers would establish settlements and fight one another and Southeastern tribes for dominance. The image above shows Ponce de León and his men fighting Florida Natives.

Rico on three ships: the *Santiago,* the *San Cristobal,* and the *Santa Maria de la Consolacion.* On April 2, 1513, Ponce de León sighted land, which he called La Florida. He became the first European to set foot on the Florida coast, claiming it for the king of Spain.

The peoples of the American Southeast experienced great traumas and disruptions as a consequence of the Europeans' arrival. The Europeans brought many diseases that resulted in epidemics in Florida and elsewhere. Death tolls varied, but smallpox, measles, yellow fever, plague, and other newly introduced diseases resulted in declining populations throughout the area. European slave raiders and warfare between Europeans and neighboring tribes caused further devastation to the Native Americans of Florida. Depopulation did not occur immediately, but by the eighteenth century, the Native population of Florida had declined by 90 to 95 percent.

Some American Indians found stability in the Catholic missions that converted them to Christianity and turned them into field workers for the Spanish. The missions promised the Native Americans religious salvation and a heavenly afterlife. Despite their presumed hopes, however, the missions hardly saved the American Indians from the upheaval of the era. Disease continued to ravage those living on the missions, and slave raiders from the north further added to the misery in Florida. By the middle of the 1700s, the American Indian population of Florida had plummeted and the Spanish mission system had deteriorated.

FLORIDA MIGRATION

Spanish officials were largely unconcerned with the number of American Indians who lived outside of the missions. Their numbers during the mission era are therefore unknown. Their descendants occupied Florida into the eighteenth century, and some would later help form the Seminole.

Other American Indians from what are now Georgia, Alabama, the Carolinas, and elsewhere also helped form the Seminole.

These newcomers migrated to Florida, often as survivors of epidemic disease, slave raids, and warfare. Although some may have come earlier, large groups began to migrate to Florida in the early eighteenth century.

Many of the migrants to Florida were Creek. The Creek were a group of American Indians who slowly formed from the survivors of many of the large chiefdoms throughout the South. This newly formed group spoke different languages (the most widespread was called Muskogee), considered themselves to be of different ethnic origins, and treated each village as a largely separate entity. Creek villages occasionally came together for a common cause—waging war, signing treaties, and negotiating trade relationships—but more often than not the Creek acted as a loose group of villages.

Other American Indian ethnicities and nationalities also came to Florida. They included Hitchiti, Mikisúkî (or Miccosukee), Yamassee, Yuchi, Choctaw, and Oconee. African-American slaves also came to Florida to find freedom from their lives as slaves elsewhere in the South. Some of these slaves became part of the Seminole villages that formed in Florida.

EUROPEAN POWER STRUGGLES IN FLORIDA

Many of the Native American migrants who would eventually form the Seminole came to Florida in the pursuit of hunting and herding grounds. The vacated lands of Florida offered tremendous opportunities. In later years, the migrants were encouraged by Spain's policy of abandoning cattle and other valuable assets upon leaving the missions, and then when it ceded Florida to the British in 1763 for control of Havana, Cuba. Great Britain and France and their respective American Indian allies had ended a long, drawn-out war—the Seven Years' War—and Great Britain now controlled all of North America east of the Mississippi, except for New Orleans.

The Spanish inhabitants and those Native Americans who had converted to Catholicism and lived in Spanish missions quickly left Spanish Florida. The British then divided the territory into

East and West Florida and began to recruit settlers to the area. Britain would rule the Florida territories until it ceded the lands back to Spain in 1783. Creek Indians—mostly Lower Creek from Georgia who were of many ethnic and linguistic backgrounds— escaped African slaves, whites, and Native Americans from other tribes—would also move to the region.

One of the first American Indians to take advantage of this opportunity was a man named Ahaya. He was first recorded as being in Florida in 1740. Soon afterward, the English began to call him "Cowkeeper," on account of the large herds of Spanish cattle that he controlled. By the 1750s, his village of Cuscowilla was near present-day Micanopy, just south of Gainesville in north central Florida. Many scholars believe that his community—the Alachua—was the first Seminole community.

Other Native American newcomers moved into long-standing villages and communities throughout the territory. In some cases, they may have joined the survivors of earlier chiefdoms, and in others they simply occupied areas and recleared farmlands that had sustained earlier peoples for centuries.

THE CREATION OF A NEW TRIBE

Despite their different tribal and cultural backgrounds, most of the newcomers to Florida slowly joined politically and socially. Marriages connected many of the newcomers—a result of social norms that frequently led men to marry women from outside of their village and move into their wives' homes. Men, in this world, traditionally returned home to teach their sisters' children how to hunt, and to participate in important ceremonies. The Florida villages also forged various political and trading ties with other American Indian neighbors. This allowed them to make better deals with the Spanish and English merchants and diplomats in the region.

The American Indian newcomers in Florida often frustrated their European and Native American neighbors. When the American Indians left Georgia and entered Spanish Florida, for example, Native American agents frequently complained that they violated treaties and dealt with competing trading firms. Spanish officials similarly worried about the autonomy that the American Indians of Florida held. Cowkeeper, for example, continued to ally himself with British traders and government officials even though he lived in the middle of territory that Spain claimed. According to some accounts, Cowkeeper pledged to be a vigilant opponent

William Bartram's Travels

William Bartram was a naturalist who traveled for several years throughout the U.S. South. He came to Florida in 1774, where he met with Ahaya, also known as Cowkeeper. Bartram's interest in writing down and otherwise recording the natural world of the Native Americans led Cowkeeper to call him "Puc-puggee," or "flower keeper."

In the following paragraphs, Bartram describes the earliest Seminole (whom he called *Siminoles*) and the environment in which they lived. Bartram describes to his readers how Florida's bounty sustained the newcomers in Florida. This is a romantic view of the Seminole and the world in which they lived. Bartram, for example, simplistically proclaims that the American Indians in Florida are an "undisturbed" part of nature, rather than recent migrants to the region.

The Siminoles [*sic*] are but a weak people with respect to numbers. . . . Yet this handful of people possesses a vast territory; all East Florida and the greatest part of West Florida, which being naturally cut and divided into thousands of islets, knolls, and eminences by the innumerable rivers, lakes, swamps, vast savannas and ponds, form so many secure retreats and temporary dwelling places, that effectually guard them from any sudden invasions: or attacks from their enemies; and being such a swampy, hommocky of Spanish authority until his death. Creek political leaders were equally frustrated by the migration into Florida. The integration of African slaves also created problems, as it angered slaveholders of all nationalities.

These frustrations led many outsiders to call the people of Florida *Seminole*—from the Spanish term *cimarron,* meaning

country, furnishes such a plenty and variety of supplies for the nourishment of varieties of animals, that I can venture to assert, that no part of the globe so abounds with wild game or creatures fit for the food of man.

Thus they enjoy a superabundance of the necessaries and conveniences of life, with the security of person and property, the two great concerns of mankind. The hide of deer, bears, tigers and wolves, together with honey, wax and other productions of the country, purchase their clothing, equipage, and domestic utensils from the whites. They seem to be free from want or desires. No cruel enemy to dread; nothing to give them disquietude, but the gradual encroachments of the white people. Thus contented and undisturbed, they appear as blithe and free as the birds of the air, and like them as volatile and active, tuneful and vociferous. The visage, action, and deportment of the Siminoles form the most striking picture of happiness in this life; joy, contentment, love, and friendship, without guile or affectation, seem inherent in them, or predominant in their vital principle, for it leaves them but with the last breath of life. It even seems imposing a constraint upon their ancient chiefs and senators, to maintain a necessary decorum and solemnity, in their public councils; not even the debility and decrepitude of extreme old age, is sufficient to erase from their visages, this youthful, joyous simplicity; but like the gray eve of a serene and calm day, a gladdening, cheering blush remains on the Western horizon after the sun is set.

"runaway." Many eighteenth-century observers called them this because they appeared to be wild and uncontrollable. The Seminole, of course, were not wild, nor were they runaways. They simply refused to let Spain, Great Britain, the United States, or the Creek national council make decisions for them. They refused to be subdued. As a result, many modern Seminole translate the term *Seminole* to mean "those who camp at a distance."

Even as the term came into use, though, a Seminole political entity did not. Throughout the eighteenth century, the American Indian residents of Florida primarily remained independent villages including Muskogee Creek, Apalachee, Oconee, and Yuchi. The Creek were divided into "upper and lower Creeks; also those they call allies and are a colony from the others living far south in east Florida," wrote Bernard Romans in his 1775 *Concise Natural History of East and West Florida*. Loyalties were to villages, clans, and kinsmen—not to tribal nations. Their relationship with northern villages slowly deteriorated, but it would not be until the nineteenth century that they completely broke.

WAVES OF MIGRANTS

American Indians from other regions continued to move into Florida between the era of the American Revolution and the War of 1812 (roughly from 1763 to 1814). The newcomers came for many reasons—economic, political, and social. Many of the migrants to Florida during these years came as a result of tensions within Creek society. Many of these tensions resulted from transformations that were leading the Creek away from long-held customs and toward something that looked like a European-style nation-state. Several powerful American Indian leaders—most notably Chief Alexander McGillivray—were attempting to centralize the Creek in order to provide a united front against white settlers and aggressive U.S. diplomats. These new leaders began to speak for more than one village, and a new national council began to act on behalf of the entire Creek people.

Soon after McGillivray died in 1793, the United States began to encourage a similar path toward centralization with what became known as the plan of civilization. The U.S. government paid Benjamin Hawkins, a former U.S. senator and Indian agent, to live full time among the Creek and to use various gifts to convince them to alter their lives. Among these changes was the ending of autonomy of villages and turning to a centralized national council to make laws for the nation.

Centralizing power into a single national council allowed the Creek to keep Americans at bay, but the costs were high. Although the nationalist leaders often profited handsomely from their new positions of leadership, they did so as local village and clan leaders saw their power stripped from them. Many Creek, who had a long tradition of village independence, blamed the leaders for violating cultural norms. Some stayed and resisted the changes; others physically moved away and weakened the reach of the national council. Native Americans who lived far from the more powerful Creek towns—and especially those who entered Florida—could withstand the pressures to cede control to the national council, and eventually the United States, which helped the council rule.

The plan of civilization had other nonpolitical components that proved equally controversial among American Indians. Hawkins urged Creek and other Native Americans to alter their daily lives. He wanted men to cease hunting and begin farming cotton and other cash crops. He wanted women, who traditionally controlled the fields, to stop farming and take care of household production. He gave women spinning wheels to turn cotton into thread, and he provided looms so they could weave fabrics for the marketplace. He gave men cattle to tend and otherwise tried to convince the Creek to become what was considered by white Americans to be "civilized."

The desires of some Creek to obtain goods that could only be purchased through the marketplace helped Hawkins's efforts. As a result, the daily lives of many Creek changed, and the American Indians began to embrace some of their white neighbors' behaviors. Some Creek owned slaves, grew and spun cotton, and fenced their lands. By 1800, many outsiders began to consider the Creek and other southeastern American Indians to be "civilized" or "semi-civilized."

These changes helped convince many American Indians to head to Florida. As the Creek began to herd more animals and grow crops like cotton to sell rather than to eat, they needed to obtain land that was not already under the control of matrilineal clans. As a result, the recently emptied lands of Florida became increasingly attractive to enterprising Creek individuals, as well as those who were frustrated by the centralization of power in Creek society.

THE RED STICK WAR

Although many Creek liked these changes, many others did not. The struggle over the transformation of their society led to a Creek civil war between 1813 and 1814. This civil war is often called the Red Stick War. This war began as a dispute among Creek, but it eventually became connected to the War of 1812 between Great Britain and the United States.

The Creek divided into two bands, each with competing hopes for the future of their nation. Red Stick Creek (often called "hostile" or "prophet" Creek because of their animosity toward the United States and their religious leadership) were largely against many of the transformations of Creek society. They allied themselves with Great Britain, which supported their cause with weapons and various other trade goods. The Red Stick represented a majority within Creek society. Their opponents were occasionally called the friendly Creek. These individuals tended to support the civilization plan and believe in the importance of the changes within Creek society. They obtained weapons and trade goods from the United States—especially from the Creek agency that Hawkins operated.

At first, the Red Stick War was contained within Creek society. Most of the fighting took place between Native Americans and within their villages. The Red Stick majority destroyed much of the property that represented the changes to their community. They freed African-American slaves, killed livestock, and destroyed cotton fields and spinning wheels within Creek villages. They even stripped some women of their European clothing to symbolize their rejection of the civilization plan. The Red Stick also attacked and threatened American Indian leaders who had ceded land or otherwise seemed to betray their villages' or communities' interest.

The Creek who had embraced some of the changes saw these actions and took flight. In the summer of 1813, many of these friendly Creek had found safety in the Alabama home of Samuel Mims, a wealthy white man who had married a Creek woman and helped Hawkins's civilization plan. On August 30 of that year, the Red Stick attacked Mims's home and the hastily erected fort on his land, freed most of the slaves, and killed about 250 of the residents inside the fort. They also took about 100 captives. Only a handful of the inhabitants who were left behind survived.

On August 30, 1813, more than 250 men, women, and children who had taken refuge at Fort Mims were killed by Red Stick warriors. This retaliatory strike on Fort Mims (*depicted above*) for a militia attack on a Red Stick supply train at Burnt Corn Creek began as people were gathering for their noon meal.

In the aftermath of the so-called Fort Mims Massacre, the United States treated the Creek's civil war as a war with the United States. General Andrew Jackson (who would later be the seventh president of the United States) marched the Army of the Tennessee, along with Cherokee, Lower Creek, and Choctaw allies, into Creek country and violently subdued the Red Stick.

On August 9, 1814, the Creek (both friendly Creek and Red Stick) were forced to sign the Treaty of Fort Jackson. This treaty required that the Creek, including those who had fought alongside Jackson, cede half of Alabama and all of their land in southern Georgia (about 23 million acres, or 9,308,000 hectares) and move west of the Mississippi River. Jackson saw no difference between the Red Stick and those who had joined his forces. The Cherokee claimed 1.9 million acres (770,000 hectares) of the 23 million acres ceded to the United States. Many of the Red Stick took flight to Florida and joined the American Indian communities there. Several of these migrants were Red Stick prophets and leaders such as Josiah Francis and Abhika. Jackson then focused his efforts on defeating the British during the War of 1812, forcing them out of Pensacola.

THE CREATION OF THE SEMINOLE NATION

With the forced migration of the American Indians out of Georgia, Native Americans in Florida were suddenly distinct from the Creek. The Creek and other migrants into Florida could no longer easily associate with the Creek communities they left behind. Instead, the migrants to Florida began to associate solely with other migrants to Florida. They married one another, celebrated ceremonies together, and traded with one another. As much as they continued to cherish the autonomy of villages and resist centralization, they had become a new people: the Seminole.

The Seminole Wars

In the first half of the nineteenth century, the Florida Seminole fought three wars with the United States. The United States waged these wars in an attempt to remove the Native Americans from Florida and otherwise end the various threats that they posed to the development of the territory and the slaveholding South as a whole. After three wars and more than $40 million of federal money spent, the wars ended in a stalemate. Thousands of Seminole were killed or removed to Indian Territory (now Oklahoma). A few hundred remained in Florida, moving from the northern panhandle to the southern panhandle in the space of a few decades.

PRIOR TO THE WARS

The migration of Red Stick Creek to Seminole society in 1814 immediately angered the United States and its Creek allies. It

also practically ensured that the U.S. military and their "friendly" Creek allies would bring the war to Florida. Indeed, shortly after the Red Stick War came to a close, General Jackson returned to Florida with his army. He came with his American Indian ally— Creek Chief William McIntosh—who brought more than a thousand warriors with him.

Together, the U.S. military and the Creek warriors waged a war of vengeance against their Red Stick enemies. They tracked down many of the fugitive leaders of the Red Stick faction, and they tried to rid the region of its British influence. In many ways, the War of 1812 and the Red Stick War continued long after they were both declared to be over.

THE FIRST SEMINOLE WAR

Although most accounts assert that the First Seminole War began in 1816 or 1817, many accounts have it starting as early as 1814. Publications by the U.S. military frequently declare that the war began in 1814, presuming little or no break between it and the War of 1812. With no formal declaration of war, no one can say for certain when the war began. Instead, historians can point to many moments of tension that flared up into violence between the United States and the Seminole of Florida.

The United States and the Creek started the First Seminole War for similar reasons. In addition to punishing their enemies from the earlier Red Stick conflict, the United States and its Creek allies also wanted to track down runaway African-American slaves and prevent their further migration to Florida. Both the Creek and the United States had growing slave populations and great reason to stop African-American slaves from finding freedom in Florida.

The fear of runaways finding freedom in Florida had a long history that dated back to the Spanish settlements in the 1600s. For more than a century, African Americans had formed separate communities in Florida and established relationships with

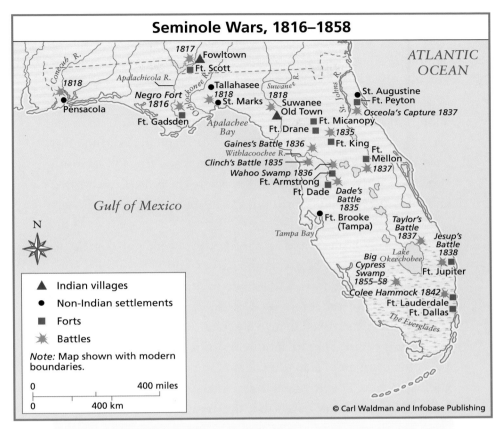

Seminole Wars, 1816–1858

1817 Fowltown

Ft. Scott

Conecuh R.

Apalachicola R.

Choctawhatchee R.

1818

Negro Fort 1816

Pensacola

Ft. Gadsden

Apalachee Bay

Tallahasee

1818 St. Marks

Suwanee

1818 Suwanee Old Town

Ft. Drane

St. Johns R.

St. Augustine

Ft. Peyton

Osceola's Capture 1837

Ft. Micanopy

1835

Ft. King

Gaines's Battle 1836

Withlacoochee R.

Clinch's Battle 1835

Wahoo Swamp 1836

Ft. Armstrong

Ft. Dade

Ft. Mellon *1837*

Gulf of Mexico

Dade's Battle 1835

Ft. Brooke (Tampa)

Tampa Bay

Taylor's Battle 1837

Jesup's Battle 1838

Big Cypress Swamp 1855–58

Lake Okeechobee

Ft. Jupiter

Colee Hammock 1842

Ft. Lauderdale

Ft. Dallas

The Everglades

ATLANTIC OCEAN

N

▲ Indian villages

● Non-Indian settlements

■ Forts

✹ Battles

Note: Map shown with modern boundaries.

0 ———————— 400 miles

0 ———————— 400 km

© Carl Waldman and Infobase Publishing

The United States fought three wars with a disparate group of Indians called the Seminoles in the first half of the nineteenth century. By the end of the third war, the Seminole who remained in Florida were reduced to about 200 people. This map shows important locations of the Seminole Wars.

neighboring American Indians. The end of the War of 1812 presented African-American slaves with the ability to protect themselves from American slave raiders. When the British left the region after the war, they decided not to destroy Fort Gibson, a fort located on Prospect Bluff near Apalachicola. Instead, they left the cannon and other weapons behind. Runaway slaves quickly occupied it, and it attracted a constant flow of newcomers. It soon became dubbed the "Negro Fort."

Although Spain technically controlled Florida, the United States was committed to destroying the fort and its presumed Seminole allies. In 1816, under order from General Andrew Jackson, the United States demanded that Spain destroy the fort. When Spain said it lacked the ability to do so, 100 U.S. troops and about 150 Creek warriors invaded the Spanish territory. Upon the arrival of the U.S. naval boats, the African Americans at the fort fired their cannon and the Americans returned fire. On its ninth shot, the United States hit the room where the powder was stored and the fort exploded. More than 250 of about 320 men at the fort were killed.

The United States and its Creek allies were not content to destroy the fort and return home. Creek and U.S. soldiers continued a campaign of tracking down fugitive slaves, stolen cattle and horses, and rebellious Red Sticks and Seminole. For several months, the mixed army marched through Native American country and tried to subdue its inhabitants. At the end of 1817, the campaign heated up again. The mixed troops targeted and destroyed Fowltown, a Miccosukee town in Georgia. Its leader, Neamathla, declared that the Treaty of Fort Jackson that the Creek had signed at the end of the Red Stick War did not affect his village. Instead, it was an autonomous village, one that neither the Creek national council nor the United States could control.

During the First Seminole War that followed, Jackson led U.S. troops and McIntosh led Creek troops into the heart of Spanish Florida. Jackson and McIntosh destroyed several Red Stick or Seminole villages. In St. Marks, which had been a trading outpost for several years, Jackson arrested two British traders for encouraging the Seminole to wage war on the United States. These traders, Robert C. Ambrister and Alexander George Arbuthnot, were both executed. Shortly after, two American Indian leaders—Josiah Francis and Homathlemico—were punished for their hostilities in the earlier Red Stick War.

Andrew Jackson's victory during the Indian wars made him immensely popular with the public. Even after he defied orders not to invade Florida in pursuit of the Seminole peoples, his success made him a national hero.

THE WAR'S AFTERMATH

The First Seminole War did little to soothe the tensions between the United States and the Seminole. It also did little to stop African-American slaves from finding refuge in Florida. As a result, hostilities between the Seminole and their white neighbors continued almost immediately after the war technically ended. The most lasting effect of the war was to convince Spain that it should cede Florida to the United States, which it did in 1821.

Soon after the United States occupied Florida, it began to address what Americans often called the "Indian problem." In 1823, it orchestrated the Treaty of Moultrie Creek. About 425 Seminole attended the negotiations, but most left when they became frustrated by the terms they were expected to accept. A few Seminole signed, and the resulting treaty declared that the Seminole would move to reserved lands in Florida and accept the protection of the United States. They would be a subdued people.

Few Seminole accepted the terms of the treaty, and most declared that it was fraudulent from the very start. The United States, however, pushed its terms onto the Seminole. The Seminole who did move south discovered that their new lands were not good for farming, and they suffered from malnutrition and starvation as a result. Although the treaty declared that the Seminole had a right to good farming lands and that the United States would provide enough supplies to get them through their first harvests, assistance from the United States did not materialize. As a result, frustrations mounted among the Seminole. Even by the terms of the flawed treaty, the Seminole felt wronged by the United States. Tensions with the United States further increased as African Americans continued to find homes in and near the Seminole communities.

A VIOLENT PEACE

Due to his victories in the Red Creek War, the War of 1812, and the First Seminole War, Andrew Jackson rose to national prominence. Known as a man of the people, he was elected president in 1828. With his presidency, the southeastern American Indian tribes came under renewed pressure to move west. This was especially true for the Seminole, who threatened the development of the recently acquired Florida territory. In 1832, the United States and Seminole agreed to the Treaty of Payne's Landing—another negotiation that many Seminole leaders immediately declared to be a fraud. Under this treaty, the Seminole agreed to move west of the Mississippi River as long as they determined that the western territories were suitable.

Once again, the United States forced the Seminole to abide by the terms of a questionable treaty and gave the Seminole three years to leave their homes for Indian Territory (now Oklahoma). The Seminole repeatedly told the agent assigned to them by the United States that they had no intention of moving west, and the agent responded by passing on word from Jackson that removal would occur peacefully or with military support.

In 1835, matters further deteriorated. Slaves continued to find refuge among the Seminole, and several former slaves served as interpreters and advisers to Seminole leaders. The most famous black adviser was a man named Abraham, a runaway slave who had adapted to the language and customs of the Muskogee Seminole. Abraham developed such a relationship with the Seminole that, according to many accounts, Chief Micanopy would not make a decision without Abraham's input.

Seminole and white settlers had many violent confrontations, with both sides declaring that their property was stolen or that they were attacked without provocation. By the end of the year, with the violence getting worse and Indian agent Wiley Thompson making it clear that he was committed to removing the Native Americans rather than protecting their interests, several Seminole began preparing to leave. Charley Emathla, one of the Seminole chiefs, sold his cattle and began to urge other Seminole to do the same and move west. Shortly after, the Seminole executed both Emathla and Thompson for betrayal.

Chief Abraham was a runaway slave who had survived the attack on the "Negro Fort." He developed a close relationship with the Muskogee Seminole and was considered a brother and ally.

With a war brewing, the United States sent in reinforcements. Just after Christmas in 1835, a detachment of 108 soldiers, with General Francis L. Dade at the lead, marched through the heart of Seminole country from one fort to another. The Seminole knew Dade's men were coming and killed all but two of them in a surprise assault. The "Dade Massacre," as it became known, began the rallying cry for the Second Seminole War.

THE SECOND SEMINOLE WAR

The Second Seminole War lasted from 1835 to 1842. It cost the United States nearly $40 million, destroyed the reputations of several U.S. generals, and took the lives of many Seminole and non-Native Americans.

The United States at first tried to march large groups of troops against the heavily outnumbered Seminole. The army had successfully used this strategy in other wars with Native Americans and presumed that it would quickly subdue the Seminole. The U.S. optimism quickly subsided as the strategy proved disastrous.

Seminole warriors fought in small parties, relying on quick and precise attacks before disappearing into the thickets of the Everglades. These tactics frustrated the U.S. Army, which suffered at the hands of a nearly invisible enemy. Over time, the United States altered its approach to the war and began to fight a campaign of attrition, or slow destruction. They would attempt to wear down Seminole families and make removal their only option.

The two most famous warriors from the Second Seminole War were Osceola and Coacoochee (also known as Wild Cat). Both obtained their positions of power in traditional ways: They proved their merit and therefore secured followings. Osceola eventually died in prison. Coacoochee, who had been captured with Osceola in 1837 but escaped and continued fighting, agreed to move west after the U.S. Army captured his daughter and wife.

While it fought a war of attrition against the Seminole—burning villages, capturing women and children, and pushing the Seminole farther into the Florida interior—the United States also waged a war against the African-American slaves in the region. The presence of former slaves and free blacks proved to be especially problematic for the United States, because African-American slaves were very reliable allies of the Seminole. As this became apparent, slaves from Florida and elsewhere increasingly took advantage of the situation to turn the war into a slave rebellion. This reality terrified white Floridians and slaveholders in general.

In 1838, Colonel Thomas Jesup used a divide-and-conquer strategy to try to separate African Americans from American Indian enemies. He offered freedom to African Americans who laid down their arms and migrated west, but promised enslavement to any

Osceola

Osceola (1804–1838) was a prominent warrior during the Second Seminole War. Prior to the war, he had been an outspoken critic of treaties with the United States, and he played an important role in the early part of the war.

Osceola was born in the Creek town of Tallassee in Alabama. He had a white trader for a father and a Creek mother; thus, by Creek rules of kinship, he was a member of a clan and the Creek tribe. Through his military achievements, Osceola earned the titles of Tustenuggee Tallassee (the Tallassee Warrior) and Tustenuggee Thlucco (Big Warrior). Like many Creek, Osceola fled to Florida after the Red Stick War. U.S. troops captured him during the First Seminole War, but he escaped and continued to fight American efforts to remove the Seminole. He was a vocal critic of the controversial Treaty of Moultrie Creek (1823). Legend has it that he put his knife through the unsigned treaty and perhaps even through the table on which it rested.

A decade later, Osceola urged the Seminole to resist the fraudulent Treaty of Payne's Landing (1832). His opposition to removal led Wiley Thompson, the U.S. Indian agent, to have him arrested. Thompson threatened to keep Osceola until he agreed to lead the Seminole west. Thompson released him only after 79 Seminole agreed to move west.

Thompson likely regretted freeing Osceola. In November 1835, Osceola helped execute Chief Charley Emathla,

African American who remained. It did not matter whether they were born free or slave, in Seminole society or on a Florida plantation: If they remained in Florida, they risked enslavement. As a result, hundreds of African Americans took the offer to move west.

a leader who decided to move west and urged others to join him. A month later, Osceola led an attack on Indian agent Thompson while other warriors attacked the U.S. military forces that were under the command of Major Francis Dade.

The so-called "Dade Massacre" officially sparked the Second Seminole War. On New Year's Eve 1835, Osceola and 250 warriors repelled a U.S. force of 800 men under General Duncan L. Clinch's command. Osceola was wounded but not severely enough to keep him out of battle.

In October 1837, several Seminole leaders believed that they could convince the United States to agree to a truce. Osceola, Coa Harjo, and 81 other Seminole traveled under a white flag to negotiate with U.S. colonel Thomas Jesup for an end to the war. Jesup ignored the rules of war and had Osceola and the other Seminole taken hostage. Osceola remained confined at Castillo San Marcos in St. Augustine until it was clear he could not be coerced into supporting removal. The army then moved him to Fort Moultrie in South Carolina, where he died on January 30, 1838.

In the aftermath of the war, Osceola became a symbol of opposition to the United States. The Seminole remembered Osceola's staunch stance against removal and the treachery that the United States used to arrest and confine him. Antislavery activists in the North also turned Osceola into an icon. His arrest under a white flag demonstrated how a war to protect the interests of slaveholders undermined American values.

Reducing the presence of African-American soldiers did not end the war. Seminole warriors continued to frustrate the United States in a series of battles—most notably the battles of Okeechobee and Loxahatchee. As a result, the United States turned to new and controversial tactics: In 1840, it began to use bloodhounds to hunt Seminole. For the rest of the war, the United States also tried to starve Seminole families into submission, burning crops, destroying abandoned Seminole villages, and otherwise preventing Seminole communities from surviving intact. They captured and ransomed Seminole women and children in exchange for promises to move west. They also began to train soldiers in amphibious warfare, hoping to take the war directly into the heart of the Everglades.

By 1842, however, the Seminole had fought the United States into a stalemate. The United States was able to capture or

For centuries, dogs were used to attack Native peoples. Hernán Cortes used ferocious war dogs to attack Aztec people of central Mexico. The American military would continue to use dogs, such as bloodhounds, against the Seminole in the Second Seminole War, which also became known as the Bloodhound War (*depicted above*).

otherwise coerce 3,824 Seminole and move them west, but the costs of continuing the war were deemed too high. The U.S. Army concluded that 1,466 soldiers and militia lost their lives as a result of the war. Many more militia members died from sickness and wounds after they returned home. The number of Seminole casualties is unknown. The number of Seminole who remained in Florida is also unknown, but most estimates are in the hundreds. Bribes, threats, bloodhounds, and hunger could not convince these Seminole survivors to migrate west. The United States estimated that only 95 men and 200 women and children remained in the state in 1842.

The United States likely underestimated the number of American Indians who remained in Florida. Nevertheless, the Seminole and the United States came to an agreement that the Seminole would maintain control of the southern portion of the territory.

THE THIRD SEMINOLE WAR

The peace that followed the Second Seminole War was relatively short-lived. Almost immediately after the war, the line that technically separated American Indians from white Floridians was routinely violated. Trade returned to the area, and sporadic violence typically followed these exchanges.

As a result, the United States initiated the Third Seminole War in 1855. After several years of unsuccessful attempts to get the Seminole to move west, the United States tried again: Secretary of War Jefferson Davis ordered a trade embargo with the Seminole and encouraged the surveying and selling of the lands in southern Florida. The United States also stationed nearly 700 soldiers in the territory.

The war began when the U.S. Army cut down banana trees belonging to Chief Billy Bowlegs. The act, which was intentionally designed to get Bowlegs to initiate an attack on American solders, worked as planned. An irate Bowlegs attacked the American forces, and the war began. Although Davis's plan convinced a few

Seminole to move west, the threats largely failed. At the end of 1855, the U.S. military increased its presence inside Seminole territory and a series of small-scale battles ensued. There were few sustained battles in the Third Seminole War and the war resulted in a few hundred Seminole being transported west. This group included Bowlegs and 40 of his warriors.

CONSEQUENCES OF THE SEMINOLE WARS

The Seminole Wars were remarkably bloody and costly for the United States and the Seminole. The United States suffered at least 1,500 casualties from the war and spent an estimated $40 million. The war also destroyed many of Florida's homesteads and plantations, limiting the development of the region. The war proved even more damaging to the Seminole. An unknown number of Seminole died in the campaigns, but the United States estimated that it caused thousands of casualties. When the Third Seminole War ended, only a few hundred Seminole remained in Florida. The rest had been transported to Indian Territory (today's Oklahoma). The Florida Seminole were unconquered, but they remained in Florida at a terrible cost.

Removals and Relocations

During the era of the Seminole Wars, the American Indians in Florida experienced a forced diaspora (permanent displacement). The Seminole found themselves spread out and increasingly divided into separate communities. Some Seminole were forcibly relocated to Indian Territory, nearly 1,000 miles (1,600 kilometers) from their birthplace in Florida. Others found themselves in the unfamiliar terrain of the Florida peninsula, a few hundred miles from the hills and forests of northern Florida and southern Georgia. Family members and neighbors were torn from each other and from the worlds they knew best.

In the years that followed, the Seminole formed two separate communities. These communities eventually became known as the Seminole Nation (in Indian Territory, before it became Oklahoma in 1907) and the Seminole Tribe (in Florida). Other Seminole moved to Mexico, the Bahamas, and elsewhere. Although they all

shared a common past and cultural heritage, the forced relocation of the Seminole helped create separate Seminole peoples. These communities and their cultures have been separated by history for almost two centuries.

THE WARS

Prior to the Seminole Wars, the United States had demanded that the Seminole return runaway African-American slaves to their owners and stop offering them safety. If the Seminole would not agree to these terms, the United States declared that removal was the best alternative. Americans believed that it was too dangerous to have the Seminole as neighbors in the slaveholding South. The fear of Seminole harboring African slaves shaped the First Seminole War, as the history of the Negro Fort demonstrates. The Second Seminole War and, to a lesser extent, the Third Seminole War also had similar motivations.

The Seminole Wars in Florida also resulted from the desire of many white Americans to take the land of the American Indians. With the expansion of cotton and African-American slavery in the early nineteenth century, obtaining land became the key to finding economic success in the United States. The entrance of Florida as a U.S. territory in 1821 made the demands for the removal of the Seminole even more severe. If Florida was to become part of the cotton-growing, slaveholding South, Americans concluded that the Seminole had to be removed.

FORCED MIGRATIONS SOUTH

In 1830, the U.S. Congress passed the Indian Removal Act. This legislation allowed President Andrew Jackson to negotiate removal treaties directly with the American Indian tribes east of the Mississippi River. The United States used this act to concoct treaties and force many of the Seminole to move west. When the Seminole refused to accept the terms of the treaties, the United States took aggressive military actions that led to the three wars. Not surprisingly, this history of fraudulent treaties and wars convinced the Seminole to be skeptical of the federal government and of outsiders in general.

During the three wars, the United States removed thousands of Seminole from their homes. The exact number is not known,

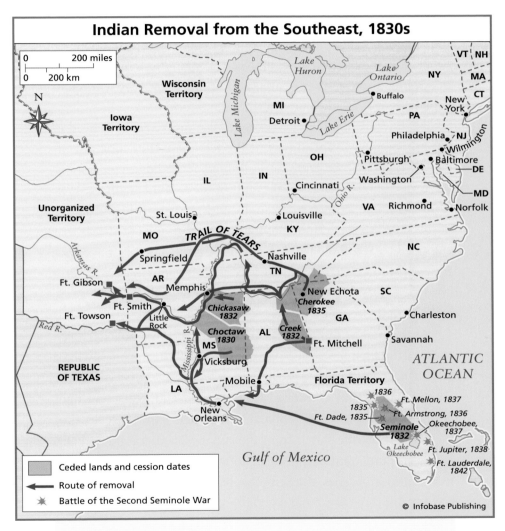

Indian Removal from the Southeast, 1830s

Beginning in 1830 and ending in 1847, the U.S. government forced the relocation of the southeastern Indians. Although the Seminole fought removal and refused to leave their land, eventually Jackson forced them to leave.

but several thousand were transported west to what was known as the Arkansas Territory, and later Indian Territory. Today, the area forms the state of Oklahoma. Many others were forced from their homes when the U.S. military invaded their villages and pushed them farther south into the Florida peninsula. Although these Seminole remained in Florida, they too experienced a forced removal. By moving south, they moved to drastically different ecosystems and away from the environment they knew and loved. As a result, they had to make many adjustments in their daily lives in order to survive. They proved to be resilient, as they learned to cope with or take advantage of their new worlds.

At the start of the First Seminole War, most Seminole lived in the northern and central part of the territory. They took advantage of the prairies to graze cattle, hunted deer, and farmed corn in the region's arable lands. At the start of the Second Seminole War, most Seminole lived farther south and far from the panhandle of the state. Men continued to herd cattle, but the cornfields that belonged to Seminole women did not flourish as they once had. Instead, women planted small gardens that contained a diverse array of vegetables, while men hunted some of the smaller game animals in the region.

At the start of the Third Seminole War, the Seminole occupied some of the least hospitable parts of the state. They primarily lived in and near the Everglades, the largest wetlands ecosystem in the United States. They continued to grow corn and beans and hunt animals. Even as they maintained ties to their past, however, they increasingly ate the starch from the coontie plant and hunted alligators and other animals peculiar to the South Florida ecosystem. In about four decades, the Seminole had adapted to three different ecosystems.

THE TRAIL OF TEARS

Most Seminole moved within Florida before finding themselves on an even longer and perhaps even more difficult journey. Indeed,

Letter from Gad Humphreys to Col. Thomas McKinney (1825)

In 1825, Indian agent Gad Humphreys wrote to Thomas McKinney at the U.S. Indian Bureau to point out the problems of resettling the Seminole on reserved lands in central Florida. Humphreys recognized that moving the Seminole to a new environment required a period of adjustment and believed that their white neighbors were unwilling to give it.

In this letter, Humphreys also makes it clear that residents of Florida needed to know that the northern edge of the Seminole territory was off-limits. In the nineteenth century, surveyors often marked boundaries by burning or slashing hundreds of trees.

Forced into unsettled conditions, the American Indians roamed throughout the country, upsetting settlers who were inclined to doubt their friendship. The settlers seized their rifles, threatened and mistreated the Seminole, and compelled them to remain permanently within the boundaries as defined by the treaty. On May 20, Humphreys wrote to the commissioner of Indian affairs about these problems:

> Sir—I have the honor to suggest that the running and making of the northern boundary of the Indian territory, is highly desirable, in order to enable me to show a line of demarcation to the white settlers, who are already thronging to the vicinity of the Indian settlements; and some, as I apprehend, have taken positions near to, if not south of, where the line will necessarily run; and will, I fear, if not expelled, become troublesome, and create disturbance among the Indians—they are squatters upon the public lands, and, of course, liable to be removed at the instance of the government, whenever it shall direct. I should be glad of instructions upon this subject.

the journey west was normally the second or third leg of a crossing that began in northern Florida, led to central Florida, and then finally resulted in a trans-American voyage west. Medicine men, clan elders, leading warriors, and women were often separated from the communities that relied on their guidance.

Some Seminole were lured west with promises of plentiful land, provisions to get them through to the first harvest, ample supplies to help with the job of clearing fields and planting crops, as well as financial compensation for their losses. These lures, however, were rarely enough to convince most Seminole to abandon their homes.

When some Seminole refused to move west, the United States found many ways to coerce them. Many of them were war captives, taken in one of the three wars and freed after their forced migration. Others left Florida after their lives were threatened or their family members were killed or captured, or when they decided that the risks of staying in Florida were too high. Some Seminole left during the wars when staying in their homelands ceased to be an option. They could move west and escape the violence of the territory, or they could move south and continue to fight for their freedom. Those families who went west took the route that is often called the Trail of Tears—a Cherokee phrase that captures the misery and trauma of the experience lived by many American Indian groups who were forced from their homes.

The forced removal of the Seminole from Florida created frustrations from the very start. In addition to the general anger and anxiety that surrounded the realities of the move, the Seminole frequently found that it was nearly impossible to bring their property with them. Some Seminole men tried to sell their cattle, but there were few buyers and prices were incredibly low. Neighboring whites recognized that they had the upper hand in the sales, and they took advantage of the situation. The indignity of the move was compounded for women. Their property, farms and gardens representing years of hard work, was unable to be moved.

The trip west was grueling. Many walked the entire way, with the few wagons and pack animals often reserved to carry supplies only. There were not even enough wagons to carry the elderly and the very young. Other Seminole took boats from Tampa Bay to New Orleans and other gulf towns before walking the rest of the way to Indian Territory. As the Seminole made their way west, their journeys typically became harder. The sick hardly healed on the march, supplies frequently ran low, and wagons frequently broke down. Medicine men tried to cure the sick, but death and disease became rampant. Elders who began the march on the wagons frequently had to walk as they got farther west.

By 1837, an estimated 46,000 Native Americans had been removed from their homeland. During their journey to the West, many Native peoples died or suffered from exposure, disease, and starvation. The route they took became known by the Cherokee as the Trail of Tears, which is depicted in this famous painting by Robert Lindneux.

The shortage of food and wagons often resulted from the greed of those hired to move the American Indians west. They lined their own pockets with handsome profits, choosing their own personal wealth over the survival of the American Indians. Kickbacks were common, and those responsible for supplying the Seminole with food and other supplies routinely overcharged government accounts. As the Seminole marched through western settlements, the white inhabitants frequently doubled the insult by harassing and stealing from the already struggling Seminole.

Death and disease was common on the march. One U.S. lieutenant declared in 1836 that the trail was full of death and misery. In McReynolds's *The Seminole,* the officer is quoted as writing "About half the party have been and are still sick. Many continue very low and must die. Three died yesterday, three this morning. It has rained powerfully every day, flooding the streams and making the roads deep and miery." Yellow fever and cholera killed many on the march, as did hunger and exposure. No families who endured the walk escaped unscathed. Death was an experience that was all too common on the Trail of Tears.

DISLOCATION

Upon their arrival west, many of the Seminole voiced their displeasure at their living conditions. They also declared that the promises that often made removal seem to be a livable option were not kept. Alligator, one of the Seminole warriors who left during the Second Seminole War, declared that he had been promised a supply of various tools and guns to replace those he and his followers had to leave behind. Without them, the men could not hunt and the women could not farm. Not only could the Seminole not eat, but the lack of supplies also prevented men and women from fulfilling their traditional roles. McReynolds quotes a man named Alligator as writing "I have no gun to kill squirrels and birds for my children." He continued by stating that he had "no axe to cut my firewood—no plows or hoes with which to till the soil for bread. . . . I am perplexed to perceive the true cause why those fair promises have not been fulfilled—or, whether they were made only to deceive me."

For the western Seminole, the years that followed removal hardly improved. In addition to the general shortages that plagued them and the problems that were inevitably related to rebuilding their lives in a new land, the Seminole also had to suffer from the indignity of living in and among Oklahoma's Creek Nation. After years of resisting the Creek efforts to incorporate them as part of the confederacy, and then fighting against Creek warriors in all three of the wars, the Seminole did not immediately receive western lands of their own. Instead they had to live in the Creek Nation. The Creek government often ignored the interests and frustrations of the Seminole. The Creek would resist efforts to allow a separate Seminole Nation until 1856.

SEPARATION

The United States did not give up its desire to remove all of the American Indians from Florida. This was apparent in all three of the Seminole Wars, but it was also evident in the years that separated the wars. In those years, the United States tried many tactics to convince the Florida Seminole that they should move west.

On several occasions, the United States tried to use the Seminole who had already come west to convince the Florida Seminole to move. In 1849, for example, after a few murders took place on the Florida frontier, Seminole Chief Coacoochee returned to Florida for the first time in about a decade. Also known as Wild Cat, the famed warrior from the Second Seminole War returned to Florida on the urging of the federal government. His job was to convince the Florida Seminole that the Seminole in the West were doing fine. Billy Bowlegs, who had fought as an ally of Wild Cat during the war, refused to meet with the former Florida war leader. Historian and Seminole Susan A. Miller, in *Coacoochee's Bones,* quotes Bowlegs as saying, "Wild Cat is my great friend! Tell him not to come out into our country until I send for him." In a short period, Bowlegs had come to see Wild Cat as an outsider to the Florida community.

When Coacoochee returned home to Indian Territory, his own frustrations mounted. Shortly afterward, he and many other western Seminole and black Seminole fled Indian Territory for Mexico. In addition to those who wound up in Indian Territory, other black Seminole escaped to the Bahamas. They settled on Andros Island during the Second Seminole War. There they escaped the war and possible enslavement. A community of descendants still lives in Andros Island today.

Adjusting to New Homes

For two decades after the Third Seminole War, the Seminole rebuilt their lives in southern Florida without significant interference from outsiders. At first, the U.S. Civil War preoccupied the United States, and the hundreds of Seminole who remained in Florida were all but forgotten by outsiders. In the late 1870s and then in the early 1880s, a few Americans encountered the Seminole again. They observed that the Seminole had survived by adapting their lives to suit the realities of the wetlands of South Florida.

The adjustments that the Seminole made largely reflected their Creek heritage and the limitations and opportunities of their surroundings. They created new forms of housing, lived in small and dispersed communities, and otherwise took advantage of the bounty provided by the Everglades. They continued to build dugout canoes and they may have relied even more heavily upon them for travel and hunting than earlier generations.

For many decades, the dugout canoe provided the most reliable form of transportation for Seminoles. They made these canoes from cypress and often used poles to traverse down the Miami River and other Florida waterways.

They harvested many of the wild plants and hunted alligators and other animals for food and hides. They also engaged in minimal trade with outsiders. They kept traders away from their villages and primarily purchased luxury items. Through all of these actions, they had formed largely self-sufficient and semipermanent communities.

DISPERSED SETTLEMENTS

Although they were often considered to be the same people by outsiders, the people known as the Florida Seminole were divided into two separate groups. They were the Miccosukee and the Seminole. It would not be until January 1962 that the United States would recognize their cultural and political distinctions. The Miccosukee tended to live at the southern edge of the Everglades and near the area that later became Tamiami Trail. As a result, they were often called Trail Seminole or Trail Indians. As noted earlier, no one knows for certain how many American Indians survived the three Seminole Wars and the relocations to Indian Territory in the nineteenth century. Scholars do, however, generally agree that the Seminole's population was roughly 300 to 400.

The two groups had many differences. Miccosukee spoke Hitchiti, and Seminole spoke Muskogee Creek. They also had different political loyalties, and according to many accounts, they had very little interaction with one another. Just as the earlier Creek custom determined, villages remained autonomous entities.

These groups were further split into communities often called bands. These bands were scattered throughout South Florida and had separate leaders. They were connected by clans and the kinship ties that were created when young adults married residents from other bands. These bands formed permanent settlements, but they also established temporary hunting camps. The postwar communities clustered into about two dozen bands that could be found near the Big Cypress, Miami River, Fish Eating Creek, Cow Creek, and Cat Fish Lake regions of Florida.

THE 1860S AND 1870S

These postwar Florida Seminole rebuilt their communities without outside interference. They were not, however, completely isolated. At first, the only contact that the Seminole had with the outside world was limited to trade and the occasional white hunter who sought assistance. Occasionally, a few Seminole men would travel to the newly settled towns of Miami and Fort Myers to trade skins or hides for boots, nails, salt, rifles, ammunition, metal goods, and other products that the Seminole could not produce themselves. These were rare events, so historians know very little about the early trading relationships. Neither white Floridians nor Seminole had any interest in learning from one another, and the white traders rarely recorded their interactions. Even more infrequent was the trade that took place in or near the Seminole villages themselves.

EARLY CONTACTS

Reconstruction—an era when much of the U.S. government's efforts were directed to rebuilding the Civil War–torn South and providing freedom to former slaves—had distracted many Americans from the presence of Seminole. When Reconstruction officially ended in 1877, the Seminole returned as a political issue. Once again, federal and state governments both advocated the removal of the Seminole to reservations west of the Mississippi River. In 1879, the federal government sent Captain R. H. Pratt into the interior of Florida to find the Seminole and convince them to move west.

Pratt believed in the benefits of assimilating the American Indians by destroying their culture and replacing it with "mainstream" American norms. For the Seminole, this required removing them from Florida and uniting them with the western Seminole, who were more integrated into American society. Despite these goals, Pratt concluded that attempts to remove the Seminole were pointless. He concluded his 1879 report by stating that only an "unworthy trick" could convince the Seminole to move.

With neither Pratt nor the federal government willing to pursue this option, Pratt's mission was a failure. A year later, the Smithsonian Institute sent Reverend Clay MacCauley to create a written account of the Seminole. MacCauley's much lengthier account remains the best-written depiction of the Seminole from the era. Perhaps more importantly, MacCauley came to Florida to understand rather than remove the Seminole. The era of forced removal was over.

A SPIRIT OF INDEPENDENCE

Pratt and MacCauley both recognized that the Florida Seminole had a fierce desire for independence. They didn't want to be told what to do by other American Indians or outsiders. This desire shaped their decision to remain divided in separate, small bands, each with its own headmen. It also led to what Pratt described as a "spirit of independence." When Pratt met with several warriors who had survived the Third Seminole War, they refused his gifts and offer of friendship. Instead, Pratt writes that the warriors stated "they could buy what they wanted." They were also wary of the strangers who wanted to enter their community. This should not be surprising, as they had endured several generations of broken treaties, treacherous military policies, and general disdain for their culture.

CHICKEES

One of the most striking changes within Seminole culture related to the homes that tribal members built. The Seminole created a new type of building that they called a chickee. This new building typically had a raised floor, no walls, and a thatched roof made of palm fronds. Built from materials that were readily available in the wetlands of Florida, the chickee was also designed to deal with the changing water levels and humidity of the area. Without walls,

The homes of the Seminole, called chickees, were efficient, functional, and easy to build. Their unique structure was especially helpful when the Seminole were pursued by the U.S. military. Today, many Seminole tribal members are building custom chickees near their modern homes for recreational and other uses.

the occupants of the homes could also enjoy whatever breeze was coming through, and slightly raised floors kept water, snakes, and other nuisances out of the way.

As much as the chickees were innovations within Seminole society, they worked with traditional settlement patterns. Seminole typically built their sleeping chickees around a common cooking

Reverend Clay MacCauley's Description of the Seminole Chickee

In 1890, the Smithsonian Institution sent Reverend Clay MacCauley to Florida to visit and write a description of the Seminole. The Florida Seminole remained a mystery to most Americans, having disappeared after the Seminole Wars into the unknown of the Everglades. MacCauley's description remains one of the best pieces of evidence historians and readers have for how the Seminole survived and remade their lives in this new environment.

In 1891, MacCauley described the chickee buildings that defined daily life for the Seminole. Although most Seminole no longer live in chickees today, many have built cooking or recreational chickees in their backyards, parks, and various other public places.

This house is approximately 16 by 9 feet in ground measurement, made almost altogether, if not wholly, of materials taken from the palmetto tree. It is actually but a platform elevated about three feet from the ground and covered with a palmetto thatched roof, the roof being not more than 12 feet above the ground at the ridge pole, or 7 at the eaves. Eight upright palmetto logs, unsplit and undressed, support the roof. Many rafters sustain the palmetto thatching. The platform is composed of split palmetto logs lying chickee—a place for the women of a clan to meet and provide for the community. The women built their own chickees around the shared cooking chickee. In essence, the Seminole built the chickees in such a way as to encourage traditional understandings of family to continue. In this manner, Seminole women literally held the community together.

transversely, flat sides up, upon beams which extend the length of the building and are lashed to the uprights by palmetto ropes, thongs, or trader's ropes.

This platform is peculiar, in that it fills the interior of the building like a floor and serves to furnish the family with a dry sitting or lying down place when, as often happens, the whole region is under water. The thatching of the roof is quite a work of art: inside, the regularity and compactness of the laying of the leaves display much skill and taste on the part of the builder; outside—with the outer layers there seems to have been less care taken than with those within—the mass of leaves of which the roof is composed is held in place and made firm by heavy logs, which, bound together in pairs, are laid upon it astride the ridge. The covering is, I was informed, water tight and durable and will resist even a violent wind. Only hurricanes can tear it off, and these are so infrequent in Southern Florida that no attempt is made to provide against them.

The Seminole's house is open on all sides and without rooms. It is, in fact, only a covered platform. The single equivalent for a room in it is the space above the joists which are extended across the building at the lower edges of the roof. In this are placed surplus food and general household effects out of use from time to time. Household utensils are usually suspended from the uprights of the building and from pronged sticks driven into the ground near by at convenient places.

PELTS, PLUMES, AND HIDES

As the nineteenth century came to an end, the Seminole of Florida increasingly participated in trade. A few traders set up camps on the periphery of the Seminole communities, but most trade continued to take place in the coastal towns of Florida. The arrival of the railroad led to the development of new coastal towns as well as access to the international marketplace. For the Seminole, this coincided with a rise of fashion trends that were in their economic favor. At the turn of the century, for example, fashion designers in New York as well as in Europe used alligator hides and egret and other bird feathers. When a ban in egret feathers went into effect in 1901, the Seminole tried to meet the growing demand for otter pelts. Seminole also traded their surplus corn, beans, and pumpkins; alligator eggs and various other eggs; beeswax; and wild fruits such as huckleberries.

The Seminole exchanged these products for a wide assortment of goods. Some were exceptionally practical and used in the obvious ways. They bought new metal pots and pans, nails for building chickees, guns and ammunition, flour, canned goods, grits, butter, sugar, coffee, and lard. In other cases, the Seminole found new uses for the items that they could find at the stores. For example, they would purchase large quantities of cheesecloth to use as mosquito netting in the wetlands. They also purchased kerosene, which when slowly burned repelled insects as well. In the late nineteenth century, Seminole women began to learn to use and then purchase sewing machines. This eventually had a tremendous impact on Seminole clothing.

RESERVATIONS

The development of coastal Florida and the Seminole's increased participation in trade brought them back into the national discussion of the nation's American Indian policy. In the early twentieth century, the federal government sought to contain rather than remove the Seminole. To this end, it began to reserve lands for them. These reservations would not be subject to surveying or sale on the marketplace. Instead, the federal government would hold the land in trust or on behalf of the tribe that permanently lived there.

In 1907, the federal government created the first reservation for the Seminole at Dania, near Fort Lauderdale in southeastern Florida. For many years, few Seminole moved there, preferring to instead stay in the more secluded interior villages. The struggles of the Seminole to get legal recognition for their lands continued in 1911. That year, the Florida Senate and House both voted overwhelmingly to reserve 100,000 acres (40,500 ha) for the Seminole. Governor William Jennings, following the logic that helped lead to the Seminole Wars, vetoed the bill. In his mind, the Seminole had already ceded their rights to Florida lands generations earlier and had committed themselves to moving west. The Florida Seminole, he asserted, belonged in Oklahoma.

Jennings lost his fight. By the end of the year, the Seminole occupied 18 separate reservations that ranged in size from about

Seminole arts and crafts are well known, especially their patchwork clothing, beaded necklaces, and handcrafted dolls. Seminole crafts were popular among early twentieth-century tourists who wanted to bring home proof of their experience with traditional Seminole culture.

40 acres (16 ha) to more than 16,000 acres (6,500 ha). These included lands that helped form the current Dania, Big Cypress, and Brighton reservations.

NEW FINANCIAL OPPORTUNITIES

In the early twentieth century, several Seminole found and created new financial opportunities in the tourist trade that had begun to transform the Florida economy. Some found items from their surroundings and others created crafts to sell to tourists who passed near their homes as they ventured to South Florida. Others participated in community events staged by city boosters in the tourist towns of Palm Beach and Miami.

This proved to be especially important after Florida began various drainage programs for the Everglades. As the water levels of the Everglades fell, the Seminole suffered. Animal communities moved, and their populations declined. At the same time, the Seminole had a much more difficult time traveling. The canoes that had once cut through the region could no longer do so as easily.

CONCLUSION

The Seminole rebuilt their communities in the decades after the Seminole Wars and their relocation to South Florida. In the process, their resiliency and adaptability allowed them to turn the Everglades into their homes. They created chickee homes and patchwork clothing, and they maintained their cultural distinctiveness. At the same time, they cautiously engaged in trade with white settlers in the region and slowly entered the tourist industry that was transforming South Florida. These endeavors provided some Seminole access to the marketplace in an increasingly fragile world.

The Crises of the Early Twentieth Century

I n the early twentieth century, the Seminole became more integrated into Florida society and its economy. After decades of
cautious and infrequent interactions, the Seminole increasingly
engaged their neighbors. The development of South Florida and
the Seminole's own need to obtain cash led to this integration.

The Seminole entered many different parts of the South Florida economy in the early part of the century. They participated in
Florida's growing tourist industry, and they traveled to take jobs
on the region's farms and often built new temporary camps near
them. They even pursued and accepted aid from the federal government. For the first time, Seminole in significant numbers also
moved to newly created reservations. These changes reflected
the Seminole's own desire to innovate and improve their lives,
as well as the dramatic changes in their local environment and
the Florida economy. By the start of World War II, the Seminole

were fully dependent on their interactions with outsiders for their survival.

ECOLOGICAL CHANGES

By the late 1910s, the Seminole could no longer rely on the pelt, plume, and hide trades. In large part this was a result of the drainage policies of the state of Florida. Starting in 1906, the government began draining the Everglades. As it built canals through the Seminole homelands, the government and private developers promoted the area as a farmer's paradise. Much of the wetlands became drier, while other areas flooded. Perhaps more importantly, outsiders bought much of the drained lands, and as

The U.S. military forced the Seminole off of their agricultural fields and into the less hospitable Everglades. The Seminole survived by adapting their life- style to suit their new ecological needs.

a result owned large sections of the Seminole hunting grounds and farmlands.

Even the natural environment did not cooperate with the Seminole's changed living conditions. In 1921, a tornado tore through the Dania Reservation, destroying many of the recently planted gardens and fields. The following year, the Seminole suffered from a drought that similarly destroyed their crops and made their homelands even drier. They had to therefore find new ways to obtain cash in order to buy their necessities. Other problems occurred during the 1930s, when the federal government destroyed the deer population because an outbreak of deer ticks threatened the state's cattle herds.

These changes made it difficult for the Seminole to rely on their surroundings for their survival. For the first two decades of the twentieth century, men continued to hunt, often selling deer meat and hides to settlers. In the years that followed, especially when deer became less plentiful, they turned to the herding of cattle. Women meanwhile engaged in planting, and the changing water levels often required that they move and clear new lands. As a result, small gardens were often supplemented by the gathering of available foods. For the families who moved to create distance from the American developments or to the newly created reservation in Dania, these changes required that Seminole women start their farms from scratch. Still, even though times were difficult, only a few Seminole looked to the Indian agency or government for financial assistance.

TOURISM

By the late 1910s, a few enterprising Seminole began to profit from the state's growing tourist market. They established new commercial villages to put Seminole life on display near the tourist hotels of Miami and Palm Beach. The most famous were Musa Isla and Henry Coppinger's Tropical Gardens, both of them in Miami.

Musa Isla and Coppinger's Gardens offered tourists similar experiences. Seminole wore traditional clothing, lived in recently built chickees, and otherwise performed daily tasks for outsiders to watch. They cooked traditional foods, demonstrated the use of the bow and arrow, carved canoes, and sewed patchwork clothing for people to wear and for the dolls that they sold. Tourists could also pay to see a Seminole woman who pretended to be an "Indian princess," a concept that did not exist within Seminole society but tourists expected to see anyway.

The villages provided a way for many Seminole families to survive the turmoil of the early twentieth century. At first, the Seminole did not receive wages, but instead took the opportunity to sell

Creating the Patchwork Tradition

At the turn of the twentieth century, the Seminole began to buy hand-cranked sewing machines. In the years that followed, they produced some of the most distinct styles of clothing in the United States. Created by tearing several colors of cloth into strips and sewing them together into various designs and patterns, the resulting patchwork clothes have come to symbolize the Florida Seminole.

The Seminole originally purchased their sewing machines from white traders at the end of the 1800s. The wives of the traders frequently taught the Seminole how to use the machines, and the Seminole women quickly became masters of them. Seminole women made all of the clothing for their families by hand, and the machines made this a less difficult task.

The invention of patchwork turned these routine tasks into jobs of great cultural significance. Some of the designs have cultural significance, but the greatest importance of the dolls, clothes, baby alligators (both stuffed and alive), toy canoes, and other curiosities. Over time, the Seminole received wages in addition to what they could earn from selling their wares. They increasingly relied on this money to buy necessities such as food, cloth, sewing machines, and various tools.

Alligator Wrestling

The highlight of the sites was alligator wrestling. The Seminole had no history of wrestling alligators prior to their participation in the tourist sites. Henry Coppinger taught the act to a few Seminole, and it took on a life of its own. Patsy West, in *Enduring Seminole,* recounted the thrill of a visitor who saw the spectacle for the first time. A Seminole, the observer wrote:

clothing is its distinctiveness. The clothing sets members of the Seminole (and Miccosukee) apart from non-Native Americans in Florida and elsewhere. Tribal members can often tell who made the clothing by looking at the designs and the craftsmanship.

In Seminole designs, a strip of a single design patch is horizontally connected to another design up and down an entire article of clothing. One shirt or blouse can have many of these strips, making the process incredibly intricate and time-consuming.

The patchwork designs helped Seminole women profit from the tourist trade in the early twentieth century. Visitors frequently purchased clothing, as well as dolls that wore the clothing, as souvenirs. In some circumstances, Seminole men agreed to participate in festivals and other events in order to allow the women to sell their sewn wares to tourists.

Today, many Seminole do not wear patchwork clothing all the time. Some do, but many reserve the clothing for special occasions, especially tribal ceremonies.

. . . [He] enters a pen of vicious alligators and with bare hands captures one, subdues it, puts it asleep, and by opening its mouth gives the visitor an opportunity to see the terrible teeth, set in jaws that are faster and more powerful than the biggest steel trap. It takes experience and daring to accomplish such a feat and is well worth going miles to see.

In 1914, Henry Coppinger opened Coppinger's Tropical Gardens, which featured a Seminole village and an alligator farm. With the drainage of the Everglades depriving the Seminole of income from animal pelts, some Seminole made a decent living at Coppinger's, offering an "authentic" Seminole experience to tourists.

At the end of the "match," an announcer would remind the audience that the wrestler was working for tips and urged them to throw money into the alligator-infested pool for the wrestler to recover. The better the performance, the better the tips.

The Tamiami Trail

The Seminole also profited from tourists who traveled the recently constructed Tamiami Trail in the late 1920s. The road cut through the Everglades, connecting Tampa on the Gulf Coast with Miami on the Atlantic. These Seminole, who would later be acknowledged as the Miccosukee Tribe, moved toward the road and set up temporary trading posts. Dressed in their colorful patchwork clothing, they sold dolls and other trinkets, had their photographs taken for small fees, and otherwise tried to capitalize on the movement of people through their homelands.

The Seminole had the upper hand in these roadside meetings. Trade occurred according to their needs; they stayed in their camps until they felt they had earned enough cash, controlled what they sold, and set their own prices. When they had earned enough cash or wanted to leave for home, they withdrew from their temporary camps, and the next wave of tourists passed through without stopping.

Pay-Per-View Events

In addition to the permanent and temporary commercial villages that they established, the Seminole also engaged the tourist market by performing mock marriage ceremonies that were concocted for the public to see. Sometimes several Seminole couples got married at the same time. At other times, tickets were sold to see the marriage of a Seminole "princess" or "chief." The Seminole also attended various festivals in South Florida, world's fairs, and other events around the country.

At these sites, the Seminole showed a combination of their real culture as well as elements that they created solely for the public eye. They wore real traditional clothing and made traditional crafts while selling tickets to public marriages and alligator wrestling. In other cases, they altered their traditional crafts or learned new skills in order to meet the demands of the tourists. Women added faces to their handmade dolls, despite a belief that doing so might bring harm to the carver. Men learned to carve peace pipes and totem poles for sale, both elements that were not original to the Seminole Tribe. They also learned to make tom-tom drums after an American Indian from Arizona taught them how.

THE GREAT DEPRESSION

In 1926, the Seminole suffered when a hurricane hit Miami and the rest of South Florida. In addition to the damage it caused to the Seminole communities, it destroyed the region's tourist market. In many ways, it brought the Great Depression to Florida a few years before the depression hit the rest of the nation in 1929.

The Seminole were in a difficult position at the start of the Great Depression. State tourism fell dramatically, minimizing the benefits of the tourist villages and the sale of crafts. The crashing economy also led many white Floridians to enter the pelt trade that the Seminole had once dominated. Indian agent Roy Nash explained in his 1931 *Survey of the Seminole Indians* that "the Indian . . . [was] regularly beaten at his own game by white men . . . who buy better traps and they take more pains in handling their pelts."

The Seminole continued to hunt, farm, and gather, but this did not provide for all of their needs. They increasingly began turning to neighboring farms for wage work. As a result, they frequently built temporary camps near agricultural fields far from their homes. They picked eggplant, peppers, green beans, tomatoes, strawberries, oranges, and whatever else was needed. Men often made the journeys to their temporary camps by themselves, leaving their wives and mothers to tend to the permanent villages that belonged to the women's clan.

The New Deal and Reservations

The federal government, under the leadership of President Franklin Delano Roosevelt, responded to the Great Depression with a series of policies called the New Deal. These programs made many improvements to people's lives, providing aid to Americans who were suffering as a result of the economy. The New Deal provided the Seminole an opportunity to call upon the assistance of the federal government. In the past, the Seminole rarely looked to the government for help. The crisis of the Great Depression changed this. In 1935, the Seminole took advantage of their participation in Palm Beach's annual celebration to make a public claim for a new reservation in Hendry County. This would become Brighton Reservation.

During the Sun Dance celebration, the Seminole issued a speech to U.S. Secretary of the Interior Harold Ickes and Commissioner of Indian Affairs John Collier. The speech, which was recorded in the 1935 Annual Narrative Report, noted that the United States and Seminole had not been at war for 100 years. Now, the Seminole explained, their future was threatened by settlers and developers. They pleaded for federal assistance and new reservations.

> We have seen them drain our lakes and waterways, cultivate our fields, harvest our forests, kill our game, and take possession of our hunting grounds and homes. We have found that it grows more and more difficult to provide food and clothing for our wives and children. We request and petition you to use your influence with Congress and the President of the United States to obtain for us the following lands and benefits.

The Seminole continued with a list of requests for titles to the lands on which they lived.

By the end of the Great Depression, the Seminole had their main reservations with boundaries that largely remain the same today (about 96,000 acres, or 39,000 ha of land). Nevertheless, the

In 1935, Mrs. Harold Ickes *(center)*, wife of the secretary of the interior, attended the Seminole Sun Dance. Here she is presented with dolls made by a Seminole woman and girl.

Seminole were not united in their call for reservations, or in their declaration that the Seminole and the United States were at peace. Many refused to move onto the reservation lands. Those who lived near the newly established Everglades National Park often resisted the call for federally recognized reservations. The park, they reasoned, would protect their lands from developers. This group was largely made up of Miccosukee. Other American Indians—primarily those of Creek background and who lived farther from the Everglades—saw reservations as essential to continuing their culture.

Reservations would create self-rule and thus allow the Seminole to choose their own cultural paths.

Job Training and Aid

During the Great Depression, the federal government provided the Seminole with some basic needs. Through several New Deal policies, the Seminole obtained various supplies from the Indian agency, including blankets, clothing, and shoes. Many of these articles were army surplus items left over from World War I.

The Seminole also received varied forms of job training. Through the Civilian Conservation Corps-Indian Division (CCC-ID), the federal government taught the Seminole many of the skills necessary to maintain the reservations. They learned about water control as well as how to maintain ranges, dig wells, and operate heavy machinery. They also learned how to restore forests and grasslands. Most of the New Deal efforts focused on the Dania Reservation, which was largely empty until 1926. Most Seminole, though, were reluctant to move to Dania, even if it offered opportunities for work and training.

In 1933, some Seminole were hired to help clear the lands on the Dania Reservation. They cleared the timber and palmetto that had fallen during the 1926 hurricane, and they otherwise made it possible for temporary visitors to camp there when they came to visit the agency. They also planted grass to turn parts of the reservation into more attractive pastures.

Livestock

During the Great Depression, the Seminole also made the transition toward widespread cattle herding. In the past they had controlled large herds of cattle, but the turmoil of war, removal, and its aftermath led to their gradual decimation. In the late 1930s, the herds began to be replenished. It began with a 1936 gift of 500 head of cattle from the Apache in Arizona, who had heard of the economic plight of the Seminole. The Seminole also obtained cattle from various governmental agencies, especially when the federal government began to eradicate the region's deer in order to end a deer tick infestation that threatened Florida's cattle herds.

During this period, the Seminole had some of their first beneficial experiences with the federal government. Rather than waging war or forcing them from their lands, the United States government shielded the Seminole from some of the misery of the Great Depression. The New Deal policies lasted until 1942, when the federal government ended the CCC-ID. With the nation turning its attention to World War II, the Seminole once again were left to their own devices to survive. A few Seminole enlisted and served with distinction in the war, but it was not until the postwar years that the tribe would become fully integrated into the national story.

The Era of Recognition

When World War II came to a close, the world that surrounded the Florida Seminole was transformed. A postwar boom brought tourists and new residents to Florida in record numbers. Thousands of American soldiers had come to South Florida to train during the war, and then returned when the war was over.

The Seminole turned this influx of newcomers into an opportunity. In addition to tourist sites at Musa Isla and Coppinger's Gardens, dozens of new sites emerged in South Florida. Some, but not all, were linked to preexisting tourist operations. For example, the Jungle Queen, a popular water tour of South Florida, added a "Seminole Village" into its itinerary.

In this postwar era, the Seminole also invested much of their efforts into becoming prominent cattle herders. This was especially true at the Big Cypress and Brighton reservations, where the

In 1936, the Seminole cattle industry began with a herd of half-starved cattle that arrived from Apache Indians. Although the Seminole were still dependent on the Bureau of Indian Affairs for assistance, the Seminole men were able to advance in other areas due to their cattle profits. Today, the Seminole Tribe is among Florida's top beef producers. (*Above*) Seminole Indians weed out unbranded cattle from the pen in 1948.

grasslands were good for grazing. Most of the herders with large stocks were men, but women became herders as well.

In some ways, the cattle herds made some Seminole dependent on the government for assistance. They looked to the Indian agency for technical assistance with the herds, as well as for financial assistance to buy more cows, feed, fences, and other necessities. At the same time, though, the herds helped the Seminole become more independent. Seminole men met to discuss technological advances in managing their stock and other issues that arose from their economic pursuits. These meetings helped many Seminole men prepare for their future roles in Seminole politics.

Seminole culture transformed in other significant ways during the 1950s. With the urging of government agents and women's groups in South Florida, the Seminole began to live in homes made of cinderblock. The homes were built to strengthen nuclear households (those consisting of a mother and father and their children) rather than the extended families of matrilineal clans. Many Seminole women were reluctant to move into the homes either because they were built too far from their maternal kin or because they were deemed less practical than the chickees. Still, the lure of the homes and their modern conveniences convinced many others to move.

After the war, the Baptist Church also became a prominent feature of Seminole life. For many decades, the Seminole had resisted the efforts of Christian missionaries to convert them to an unfamiliar set of beliefs and customs. Starting in the 1940s, however, Seminole Christian missionaries from Indian Territory began to preach and seek out converts in Florida. These missionaries had much better success than earlier ones, and they gradually converted members of the Florida communities. They held services in the Muskogee and Hitchiti languages, and the Seminole Baptists frequently merged their new Christian beliefs with their traditional understandings of the cosmological world.

NEW ATTITUDES TO GOVERNMENT

With these changes, the Seminole's approach to the federal government and their non-American Indian neighbors changed. The transformation began during the New Deal and became clearer in the war's aftermath. Although the Seminole were still skeptical of government motives and of outsiders in general, they relied on outsiders to obtain many of the resources and skills that they needed to prosper economically and politically. A few children attended special boarding schools designed for American Indian children. Others received tutoring or basic education from various so-called "Friends of the Seminole" groups.

The Seminole's attitude toward their own government changed as well. During this era, Seminole leaders from across Florida began to meet and discuss topics of common interest for the first time. Although it was not a national council or a formal government, the meetings served the function of a tribal council. They met on the Dania Reservation under a huge oak tree. These meetings helped unite the diverse groups into a loosely defined community.

INDIAN TERMINATION POLICY

The meetings under the oak tree helped prepare the Seminole for the shock that came when they heard about an impending policy from Congress, called Termination. The U.S. government proposed to "terminate," or end, its special relationship with Native Americans and to assimilate them into mainstream society. Native Americans would be granted the rights and privileges of citizenship, and their dependency on government programs would be reduced. This policy was a reaction to the New Deal policies that strengthened tribal authority and encouraged cultural diversity. Throughout the New Deal, for example, the federal government helped the Seminole with health care, education, and various economic development projects. According to New Deal policy makers, the government would not turn the Seminole into typical U.S. citizens; it wanted instead to help allow the Seminole be self-sufficient.

The postwar mood in the nation concluded that these policies needed to come to an end. Conservatives wanted to eliminate reservations because they were seen as barriers to the ultimate assimilation of American Indians into U.S. society. Many liberals wanted the policies to end, largely because they were seen as destructive intrusions.

When word reached the Seminole that they might lose federal assistance, the various Seminole communities responded. The leaders who had been meeting at the oak tree decided that they needed to send a delegation of representatives to appear before Congress and make their voices heard. Often led by the women of the communities, the Seminole began to organize and raise money for this venture into national politics. One of the fund-raisers was a rodeo, an event so successful that the Seminole have continued to hold similar events for the public ever since.

In 1954, eight Seminole traveled to Washington, D.C., to meet with Congress. They represented an estimated 625 of the 900 American Indians in the state of Florida. Most of the 625 lived on a reservation. The 275 Seminole whose interests were not represented by the group were frequently of Miccosukee backgrounds, and they often lived off the reservations and near Tamiami Trail.

The delegation submitted a prepared statement to Congress. In it, the Seminole declared that they were not ready for self-rule. They lacked an educated leadership, suffered from various health problems, and needed federal help to finish the drainage and conservation projects on the reservations. They asked for 25 years of continued assistance before any future decision would be made about their tribal situation. Their report, which was recorded in Congress's *Termination of Supervision,* stated that "[d]uring the past 20 years our advancement has been rapid, but we need guidance for a longer period and we look to the Federal Government for continuance of their supervision."

The Seminole optimistically believed that government assistance would eventually lead to self-determination and economic prosperity. When questioned by the government committee about the sort of progress that would be possible in 25 years, Laura Mae Osceola declared that there were no limits as to what the Seminole could achieve. "In 25 more years they won't need your help. We will be giving you help!"

On December 19, 1954, U.S. Commissioner of Indian Affairs Glenn Emmons (*standing*) represented President Eisenhower at a meeting with the Miccosukee Seminole in the Everglades. Buffalo Tiger sat at the right of Emmons, and the Miccosukee's attorney, Morton Silver, sat to Emmons's left. The Miccosukee wanted a pledge that the U.S. government would protect their rights to hunt and live in villages without interference from whites.

Meanwhile, the Miccosukee proclaimed that they were a separate group and should not be treated as part of the Seminole. In addition to meeting on their own with the committee, they presented an aide to President Dwight D. Eisenhower with the Buckskin Proclamation. This pronouncement, written on a hide with egret feathers, declared that the Miccosukee were a distinct group that wanted to live independently from the Seminole and the federal government. The Miccosukee said that they would not deal with the Bureau of Indian Affairs; they would deal only with a representative of the president.

The Seminole left Washington with their future still in doubt. In 1955, the committee met in Florida and took the testimony of many Seminole, employees of the Indian agency, as well as neighbors familiar with the American Indians. The committee also met with representatives of the Miccosukee from the United Seminole Affairs Association of Miami. The association included Buffalo Tiger and Ingraham Billie, a medicine man who was looked upon as one of the most knowledgeable members of the tribe.

The lobbying—by both Seminole and Miccosukee—convinced the committee to take the Seminole off of the list. Many members of the committee were either confused by the divisions among the Seminole or convinced that they were too disorganized to act independently of federal aid.

THE SEMINOLE RECEIVE RECOGNITION

The experience of fighting against Termination led many Seminole to conclude that they needed a more permanent way to protect themselves. They decided to organize themselves as a formal government and apply for federal recognition as a tribal government. Many Miccosukee split from this movement, including Buffalo Tiger and Ingraham Billie. Nevertheless, a committee of seven Seminole created a constitution and government. There were two representatives from each of the three reservations, as well as a Miccosukee representative.

A corporate charter was issued to the Seminole in June 1957. Two months later, on August 21, 1957, the Seminole voted to approve a constitution and bylaws as well as the charter. The votes were overwhelmingly in favor: The constitution passed by 241 votes to 5; the charter passed by 223 to 5. Through these acts, the Seminole Tribe of Florida was formally created. The following year, 1,025 Seminole were enrolled as members in the new tribe.

The creation of the Seminole Tribe angered Tiger and other Miccosukee. Because the federal government refused to acknowledge the distinctions between the two groups, the Miccosukee were not subject to the Seminole council. Not surprisingly, then,

Buffalo Tiger on the Termination Hearings

Buffalo Tiger, one of the leaders of the Miccosukee in Florida, served as one of the group's main spokespersons during the 1954 Congressional hearings. Tiger was chosen by Miccosukee elders because of his ability to speak English and his shared belief that Seminole recognition would harm the Miccosukee. Tiger's testimony brought confusion to the room. He declared that the Miccosukee and Seminole were separate communities, and he objected to the federal government's and the Seminole's willingness to create a single tribe out of two separate people. Few congressmen understood that the Miccosukee considered themselves to be separate from the Seminole. Even fewer could understand the Miccosukee stance that they wanted nothing from the government but to be left alone.

In the following excerpt from Tiger's memoir, he recalls what the Miccosukee wanted from the hearings. Whereas the Seminole wanted 25 years to prepare for assimilation into American society, the Miccosukee wanted to live a tribal life forever.

> We wanted to make sure that the Indian Bureau and government in Washington listened to us and understood how our feelings are for Miccosukee people. So I didn't have an easy job.

the Miccosukee continued to pursue their separate recognition long after the fight against Termination ended.

At first, the Miccosukee's claims were generally dismissed. They could not convince the president, the new Seminole council, or representatives of the Bureau of Indian Affairs of their separateness. These parties all rejected the claim that Miccosukee were a

We found out that we had to go to Washington, but before that I had to get some type of help like a lawyer that understood that type of business because I was just a young guy who didn't know too much of anything. In fact, I didn't know the Bureau of Indian Affairs was in Washington. But our leaders, those people we call medicine men, they had selected us to go up there and make sure that nothing happened to us. In other words, we were not asking for anything.

We were not telling the government what we wanted; we didn't want anything from them. That was my job: to let them know we were not too concerned about education and welfare and all the things that tribal reservation people usually had to work with. We didn't have a reservation; we never wanted it. We really didn't care about that type of life at that particular time. The medicine men who selected me to speak for them were so particular about not taking anything from the white man, not even ten cents, and not accepting anything from them. So I'd always go back and tell them this is what Washington wants us to do. If they said yes, we could do it, I would say yes. In other words, I was taking strict orders. . . .

We just wanted to live our life. We just wanted to live on the land the way we had always lived on it—to hunt and find food the way we had always done it. We didn't want anything new, any new ideas; we didn't want that. So that's what made us want to go up there.

separate tribe. Instead, they treated the Miccosukee as a distinct part of the Seminole Tribe. The federal government was not about to recognize a new tribe when it was doing its best to end its obligations to other American Indian groups.

In 1959, a group of 11 Miccosukee representatives took matters into their own hands. They flew to Cuba and met with

On August 21, 1957, Seminole Indians M. Sam Huff, 94, (*left*) and Louise Billie, 71, (*right*) cast their ballots to vote whether or not to adopt a tribal form of government at the Dania Reservation. The constitution and charter passed, officially creating the Seminole Tribe of Florida.

Communist leader Fidel Castro, who had just claimed power in Cuba by ousting a supporter of the United States. While they were in Havana, the Miccosukee used an eighteenth-century treaty with Spain to support their claims as a sovereign nation and created a formal relationship with the Cuban government.

The Miccosukee's trip to Havana was an embarrassment to the United States. It attracted the ire of both U.S. and Seminole officials. Some Florida legislators were so upset that they publicly reconsidered an offer to give reservation status and other aid to the Miccosukee. Representatives of the Seminole repeatedly made it clear that the 11 Miccosukee did not speak for them.

Despite the anger it produced, the trip to Havana convinced the United States to recognize the Miccosukee. The Bureau of Indian Affairs helped the Miccosukee create a constitution and apply for federal recognition. In 1962, after a few years of delay, John F. Kennedy's administration took up the issue. In the vote to ratify the Miccosukee constitution, 66 of the 94 eligible Miccosukee voters voted; the tally was 58 in favor and 8 opposed. The Miccosukee had secured their separate status from the Seminole. Soon after, Tiger was elected as the first tribal chair.

The Seminole and Miccosukee both put meaning behind their newly won relationships with the federal government. Betty Mae Tiger Jumper, the Seminole chairwoman from 1967 to 1971, explained this in her memoir *A Seminole Legend*: "When we became organized, we took steps forward to fight in the white man's world at tables, instead of with bows and arrows and guns. We learned how to fight in such a manner that things began coming our way." The Seminole applied for grants, forged alliances with neighboring environmental and civil rights groups, and otherwise pursued what they believed were their best interests.

The Modern Transformation

S ince 1957, the Seminole have undergone one of the most interesting transitions in American Indian history. In only a few decades, the Seminole went from being seen as the last remnants of an unconquered and uncivilized tribe to one of the most highly visible tribes in the United States and the global marketplace. Where once they suffered from poverty and disease, they are now national leaders in the legal fight for tribal independence. Where once they looked to the federal government and private employers for employment, they are now creators of jobs and employers of thousands of workers in Florida and abroad. Today, they are among the most powerful political and economic leaders in the state of Florida, and they are also important players in the global economy. Few communities have made this transition so quickly and completely.

Economic and political power has not destroyed Seminole culture. On the contrary, the Seminole have experienced a cultural revitalization movement. Through various institutions and tribal programs, the Seminole Tribe of Florida has focused its attention on teaching the Hitchiti and Muskogee Creek languages, teaching patchwork and other crafts to their children, and encouraging their communities to integrate the traditional with the modern. The tribe has used its legal independence to incorporate tribal ideas of justice into its legal system and traditional medicines within its health department and programs. Although virtually all Seminole live in modern-style homes, many of them have also built or purchased chickees for their yards. Wealth and power have allowed the Seminole to reinvigorate their communities and their culture.

SEMINOLE CULTURE AFTER RECOGNITION

Tribal independence did not immediately change the daily lives of most Seminole. In the late 1950s through the 1970s, most Seminole lived much as their parents had lived. A survey taken in 1963 revealed that 99 of 175 Seminole families earned less than $500 per year. If anything, the Seminole during these decades experienced unprecedented cultural assimilation. A few Seminole engaged in the tourist trade or herded cattle, but most found wage labor jobs at industrial and agricultural sites in South Florida.

Many of the developments that transformed Seminole society in the middle of the twentieth century contradicted earlier cultural norms. Many jobs, for example, required men and sometimes families to move away from their clans. Men had traditionally traveled away from their families to hunt game, but the new obligations of industrial and agricultural work were different. Many Seminole traveled by themselves, and few jobs allowed the workers to return to their homes to participate in multiday rituals such as the Green Corn Ceremony.

Florida's secondary schools as well as the Baptist preachers who preached to the Seminole Tribe also helped encourage assimilation into mainstream Florida society. Both schools and churches took hostile approaches to traditional knowledge, even as the Seminole increasingly turned to these institutions as paths to self-improvement. According to some sources, attendance at the Green Corn Ceremony declined while traditional ways of life were pushed aside.

TOWARD SELF-SUFFICIENCY

Between the 1950s and the 1970s, the Seminole made many efforts to become self-sufficient. Almost immediately after the Seminole Tribe ratified its constitution in 1957, they began to plan the building of their own commercial village. The Okalee Indian Village opened in 1960 on the Hollywood Reservation (formerly known as the Dania Reservation). It featured many of the attractions that characterized Musa Isla and the other outsider-run enterprises in Florida. The Okalee Indian Village offered alligator wrestling, mock weddings, and the ability to watch Native Americans create various crafts that could then be purchased. When Musa Isla and Coppinger's Tropical Gardens closed in the 1960s—largely due to the building of a highway that made access to the sites incredibly difficult—the Okalee Indian Village obtained a near monopoly on the tourist trade.

The tribal council created several other economic ventures during these years. One of the most well known is Billie's Swamp Safari, an airboat tour of the Everglades that continues to run to this day. The Seminole had served as hunting guides for more than a century, but the airboat rides offered something different. Hunting guides in the early twentieth century found sporadic work from only a few willing hunters. The airboat rides continue to attract thousands of tourists looking for a couple of hours of entertainment. They come to see the American Indian homelands, in addition to the alligators, herons, egrets, and other wildlife that make the Everglades their home. The tours occur regularly— many times a day—and they have provided a consistent source of revenue for several decades.

Other significant changes occurred after the Seminole's federal recognition. The migration of bands to the reservations increased dramatically in the 1960s and 1970s. Much of this migration occurred when the Seminole lost their lands to South Florida developers.

Today, visitors to the Everglades can tour the land of the Seminole aboard customized motorized airboats at Billie's Swamp Safari. These tours of Seminole chickee villages, a nature trail, and reptile shows and bird exhibits have provided a consistent source of income for decades.

Many others, though, came to the reservations to take advantage of the minimal resources and programs provided by the tribal council. The council found some grants and leased some of their lands to local ranchers in order to raise money and hire their citizens to improve their conditions. These financial gains were small, amounting to only a few hundred dollars for each Seminole family. Culturally, however, the tribal council began to push for reforms that allowed the Seminole to make their own decisions about their daily lives.

THE TRANSFORMATION OF SOUTH FLORIDA

The biggest changes for the Seminole resulted, at least in part, from the transformation of South Florida. The Seminole had originally
(continues on page 100)

Betty Mae Tiger Jumper
(born 1923)

In 1967, Betty Mae Tiger Jumper was elected the first female Seminole chief. She also was awarded an honorary doctorate by Florida State University.

Betty Mae Tiger Jumper was born in South Florida's Indian-town but moved to the Dania (Hollywood) Reservation shortly after her birth. In 1967, she became the first woman to be chief of the Seminole Tribe of Florida. That made her the first female chief of a federally recognized tribe.

Jumper was part of a generation of Seminole who learned to bridge tradition with the modern world. She attended the Cherokee Indian School in North Carolina and was the first Seminole to earn a high school diploma. Many members of her family disapproved of her pursuit of education and her decision to leave her home to get it. Before she left for the boarding school, she spoke Mikasuki and Muskogee Creek, but not English. This would quickly change at school.

In 1946, she married the founder of the Seminole Tribe of Florida, Moses Jumper, who had just returned home from service in World War II. She worked as a nurse at a Miami hospital for a short while, before becoming a nurse for the dispersed Seminole communities. She headed up the Seminole's health department for many years and helped bring both modern and traditional health care to her people. Jumper was the first vice chairperson of the tribe, serving immediately after the tribe obtained federal recognition in 1957.

Jumper served as Seminole chief from 1967 to 1971. Under her watch, she leased land to non-Seminoles to fill the coffers of the Seminole treasury. In addition to her valuable work for the tribe, she also sat on many local and national committees. In 1970, President Richard Nixon appointed her to the National Congress on Indian Opportunity.

Jumper has spent her life serving her community. In addition to her work in improving the health of her community, she has also served as the editor of the *Alligator Times,* a newspaper that later became the *Seminole Tribune.* Jumper is also known as a Seminole storyteller. Her stories and her autobiography have been published as *Legends of the Seminole* (1994) and *A Seminole Legend: The Life of Betty Mae Jumper* (2001).

(*continued from page 97*)
resettled in South Florida because many Americans had determined that the terrain was unsuitable for them. In the 1960s and
1970s, after the widespread introduction of air conditioning and
the national growth of sunbelt cities, this changed. Between 1950
and 1980, for example, Miami's population went from 693,705 to
3,220,844. Other areas of Florida experienced similar if not even
greater population explosions. During the same span of years,
Broward County, which contains the Hollywood Reservation,
went from 83,933 to 1,018,200.

The population explosion in South Florida changed the daily
realities and opportunities for the Seminole. In many ways, this
transformation presented yet another crisis for them. Residents of
the Hollywood Reservation, for example, found themselves living
near many of the newly created or recently expanded suburbs of
Fort Lauderdale. These communities threatened the Seminole's
prized isolation, presented all of the vices and temptations of
the era, and otherwise offered tribal members countless ways to
assimilate. Once again, however, the Seminole turned the crisis
into opportunities.

SMOKE SHOPS

The Seminole's path to economic success first began when they
leased some of their prized lands to ranchers in the 1960s. Their
success became even greater in 1977, when Chief Howard Tommie
convinced the Seminole Tribe to begin selling discount cigarettes.
Because the Seminole did not have to collect taxes on products
sold on tribal lands, they could charge less than their non-Native
American neighbors. For most items, the sales tax was too low to
benefit. Cigarettes were different. The Seminole could sell a carton
of cigarettes for $5.50 and not charge the additional $2.10 in taxes.

The Seminole opened their first of six drive-through smoke
shops on a small plot of land they had received years earlier in
exchange for allowing the state to build the Florida Turnpike

through the heart of the Hollywood Reservation. When the Seminole received the plot, the land was widely considered worthless. As South Florida developed, however, the plot became remarkably valuable. It was adjacent to a road that became a major thruway in greater Fort Lauderdale and was a short distance away from the growing population centers of South Florida.

The sale of discount cigarettes allowed the Seminole to take an important step toward self-determination. It taught them valuable lessons on how to use their tribal independence. The Seminole would fight many cases regarding water rights and other issues in the years that followed. They also became the national leader in the struggle for what might be considered the most important economic issue in modern American Indian history: gaming.

THE 1980S AND BINGO

The jump from tax-free cigarettes to high-stakes bingo as a moneymaker occured relatively quickly. Bingo was already legal in Florida in 1980. Nonprofit groups across the state could operate the game as long as they limited jackpots to $100 and followed various regulations. When the Seminole opened their first bingo hall at the Hollywood Reservation in 1980, few realized the magnitude of the decision. The venture was successful, largely because the Seminole offered a jackpot of $1,000.

Matters came to a boil when Broward County sheriff Bob Butterworth ordered the operation to be shut down. Seminole leaders claimed that tribal independence freed them from the regulations of the state. Butterworth and others disagreed. The landmark decision *Seminole Tribe of Florida v. Butterworth* agreed with the Seminole. The U.S. Circuit Court of Appeals thus set the stage for the national emergence of tribal gaming. In 1988, the federal government put much of the *Seminole v. Butterworth* decision into legal code with the Indian Gaming Regulatory Act (IGRA). This act, which is still in effect today, set federal guidelines to determine the limits to legalized gaming on tribal lands.

After Congress passed the IGRA, the Seminole slowly expanded their gaming offerings on the reservations. In the early 1990s, they began to install video bingo and other electronic games. The following decade, they forged ties with the corporation Hard Rock International to build casinos on the Tampa Bay and Hollywood reservations. Two Seminole Hard Rock Hotel and Casinos opened in 2004, one in Hollywood and the other in Tampa. Over time, these and other smaller casinos on the other reservations became the most important economic venture of the tribe. Individuals continued to herd cattle—especially those who lived at Big Cypress or Brighton—but the tribe itself began to rely on casino wealth.

In 2006, the Seminole Tribe of Florida bought Hard Rock International for $965 million. This international deal included 124 Hard Rock Cafes, as well as several hotels and casinos in the United States and abroad.

In December 2006, the Seminole Tribe of Florida took the next step in the expansion of its financial empire: It purchased Hard Rock International for nearly $1 billion. This purchase, like all other ventures, carried some risk. So far, it has seemed to pay off.

THE CULTURE THAT CASINOS SAVED

With their newly created wealth, the Seminole have embarked on a campaign to protect and reinvigorate their culture. In *High Stakes: Florida Seminole Gaming and Sovereignty* (2008), anthropologist Jessica Cattelino concludes that the newly created Seminole wealth has resulted in a cultural renaissance. The Seminole are no longer struggling to survive or find ways to assimilate into the American norm. Instead, they are using the wealth generated by casinos and other economic ventures to maintain their traditions.

The Seminole's success in their modern economic ventures has allowed the tribe to offer a new sense of security to its members. The tribe makes monthly payments to its citizens and offers a wide range of social services. It has a housing department that helps with home repairs for all members and offers loans to citizens. It funds a tribal newspaper (the *Seminole Tribune*) and a broadcasting network.

Perhaps most importantly, the tribe provides health services for all of its citizens. Employees of its health department use traditional healing methods alongside modern medical practices as defined by the American Medical Association. In this manner, the modern and the traditional complement rather than contradict one another.

One of the most remarkable ventures that the Seminole have created is the Ah-Tah-Thi-Ki Museum on the Big Cypress Reservation. This state-of-the-art museum opened in 1997, and in 2009 it received accreditation from the American Association of Museums. It is the first tribal museum to receive this distinction. The museum contains 5,000 square feet (465 square meters) of exhibit space and a 1.2-mile (2-kilometer) boardwalk that extends into the cypress swamp to ceremonial grounds and a living village. Visitors learn about the art, history, and culture of the Seminole through interactive as well as traditional exhibits.

The Seminole have also turned to casino wealth to reinvigo-rate their educational programs. In addition to the museum and an active senior center, the Seminole have established scholarships for their citizens to attend postsecondary school. They have also started their own schools. On the Big Cypress Reservation, they run the Ahfachkee Day School. The Seminole also run a char-ter school on the Brighton Reservation, the Pemayetv Emahakv Charter School. Seminole schools integrate traditional language and crafts while mandating high standards for reading, writing, and arithmetic. Seminole history and culture permeate the cur-riculum: Students learn about traditional medicines; they learn geometry by examining the structure of a chickee; and they say the Pledge of Allegiance to the U.S. flag in their own language as well as in English.

The revitalization of Seminole culture has also occurred through various community events. Groups of Seminole attend a wide range of cultural and sporting events in South Florida: They go to Dolphins football games and watch from a tribal box. They have an annual "rez rally" to raise money for diabetes research. They have their own sporting leagues, and they sponsor trips to historical, cultural, and other desirable destinations. Casino wealth has once again allowed the Seminole to act as a traditional community, often in fundamentally modern ways.

CONTEMPORARY SOCIETY

In 2010, nearly 200 years after the First Seminole War began, the Seminole have more than just survived. There are more than 3,330 enrolled members of the Seminole Tribe of Florida. They primar-ily live on one of six reservations in the state, although most live on the three largest and oldest ones: Big Cypress, Brighton, and Holly-wood. The other three—Tampa, Immokolee, and Fort Pierce—

have very small populations or are primarily sites for economic development. At the same time, there are about 550 members of the Miccosukee Tribe and more than 15,500 enrolled members of the Seminole Nation in Oklahoma.

In recent years, the Florida Seminole have led the national fight to protect Native American independence and they have become a nationally, if not internationally, recognized American Indian tribe. With revenue generated by gaming and other economic ventures, the Seminole have brought their historical experiences and cultural values into their classrooms, doctors' offices, public festivals, and housing policies. In the process, they have revitalized their community and defined, on their own terms, what it means to be a Seminole.

The Seminole's path from the hills and prairies of northern Florida to the present has been more than tumultuous. They have survived three wars, the constant rebuilding of communities, and the miseries and frustrations of constant poverty. Today, as contemporary realities offer a much more optimistic hope for the future, the Seminole remember these parts of their history and pride themselves in their "unconquered" heritage.

Chronology

XYXYXYXYXYXYX

1513 Spaniards under Ponce de León's leadership claim the southeast of North America and call it *La Florida*.

1740 Cowkeeper establishes Cuscowilla, an Alachua town near present-day Micanopy in north central Florida.

1763 Spain cedes Florida to England as part of the post–Seven Years' War settlement.

1783 England cedes Florida to Spain, which had conquered part of the territory two years earlier.

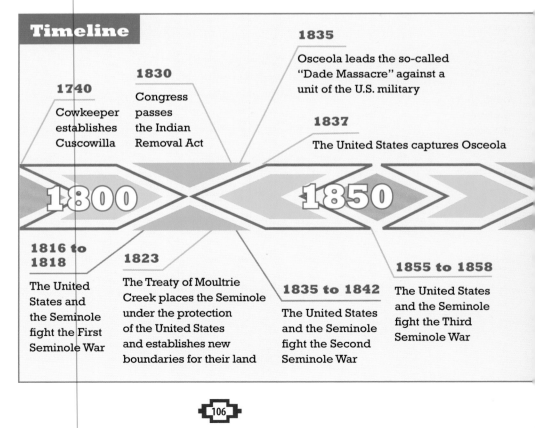

Timeline

1835
Osceola leads the so-called "Dade Massacre" against a unit of the U.S. military

1830
Congress passes the Indian Removal Act

1740
Cowkeeper establishes Cuscowilla

1837
The United States captures Osceola

1800 **1850**

1816 to 1818
The United States and the Seminole fight the First Seminole War

1823
The Treaty of Moultrie Creek places the Seminole under the protection of the United States and establishes new boundaries for their land

1835 to 1842
The United States and the Seminole fight the Second Seminole War

1855 to 1858
The United States and the Seminole fight the Third Seminole War

1813 to 1814   Red Stick War divides the Creek and leads many Native Americans to flee to Florida.

1814   Creek sign Treaty of Fort Jackson to end the Red Stick War. The Creek cede their land in Georgia.

1816   The United States destroys the "Negro Fort" in Florida, ending its role as a refuge for runaway slaves.

1816 to 1818   The United States and the Seminole fight the First Seminole War.

1817   The United States destroys the Miccosukee town of Fowltown in Georgia, and the war escalates.

1821   Spain cedes Florida to the United States through the Adams-Onís Treaty.

1823   The Treaty of Moultrie Creek establishes the first treaty between the United States and some Seminole chiefs. It places the Seminole under the protection of the United

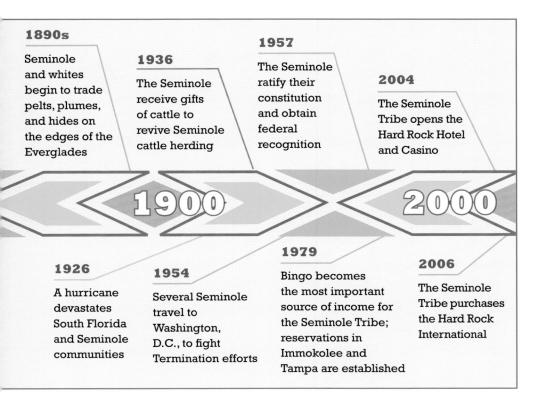

1890s

Seminole and whites begin to trade pelts, plumes, and hides on the edges of the Everglades

1936

The Seminole receive gifts of cattle to revive Seminole cattle herding

1957

The Seminole ratify their constitution and obtain federal recognition

2004

The Seminole Tribe opens the Hard Rock Hotel and Casino

1926

A hurricane devastates South Florida and Seminole communities

1954

Several Seminole travel to Washington, D.C., to fight Termination efforts

1979

Bingo becomes the most important source of income for the Seminole Tribe; reservations in Immokolee and Tampa are established

2006

The Seminole Tribe purchases the Hard Rock International

States and establishes new boundaries for their land (about 4 million acres, or 1,620,000 ha in central Florida).

1828 The United States elects Andrew Jackson, a proponent of removal, as the seventh U.S. president.

1830 Congress authorizes the president of the United States to negotiate removal treaties directly with American Indians when it passes the Indian Removal Act. Thousands of Seminole are removed from their homes, leading to more conflicts.

1832 The United States and some Seminole chiefs sign the Treaty of Payne's Landing, which includes a promise to move west to Indian Territory. Seminole leaders immediately declare after the negotiations that they had not made these promises and that they would refuse to move.

1835 Seminole war leader Osceola leads the so-called "Dade Massacre" against a unit of the U.S. military that was in Florida to subdue and remove the Seminole. It is the spark that starts the Second Seminole War.

1835 to 1842 The United States and the Seminole fight the Second Seminole War.

1837 The United States captures Osceola when he comes to negotiate under a white flag.

1855 to 1858 The United States and the Seminole fight the Third Seminole War, the last sustained effort to force the American Indians out of Florida.

1879 Captain R. H. Pratt investigates to see whether it is possible to convince the Seminole to move to Indian Territory. He concludes that he cannot.

1890s Seminole and whites begin to trade pelts, plumes, and hides on the edges of the Everglades.

1926 A hurricane devastates South Florida and Seminole communities.

1928 The United States completes the Tamiami Trail through the Everglades, bringing tourists to the Seminole and Miccosukee.

1936	The Seminole receive gifts of cattle to revive Seminole cattle herding.
1954	Several Seminole travel to Washington, D.C., to fight Termination efforts to eliminate their communal and tribal rights.
1957	Seminole voters ratify their constitution and obtain federal recognition. Billy Osceola is the first elected chairperson; Betty Mae Jumper is the vice chairperson.
1959	Buffalo Tiger and other Miccosukee representatives fly to Cuba and meet with Fidel Castro in an effort to get tribal recognition.
1962	Miccosukee Tribe of Florida gains federal recognition separately from the Seminole Tribe.
1967	Betty Mae Jumper is elected chairwoman of the Seminole Tribe. She becomes the first women to be elected chief of a federally recognized tribe in the United States.
1971	Howard Tommie is elected chairman. He helps the Seminole use their tribal independence to find financial opportunities.
1977	The Seminole Tribe begins to sell tax-free cigarettes.
1979	Bingo becomes the most important source of income for the Seminole Tribe. Reservations in Immokolee and Tampa are established.
1981	The Seminole win a federal appellate court case in *Seminole Tribe of Florida v. Butterworth*. It establishes the Seminole's sovereign rights and establishes a national precedent for tribal participation in bingo and other forms of gambling.
1996	A reservation is established at Fort Pierce.
1997	The Ah-Tah-Thi-Ki Museum opens on the Big Cypress Reservation.
2004	The Seminole Tribe opens the Hard Rock Hotel and Casino at Tampa and Hollywood.
2006	The Seminole Tribe purchases Hard Rock International.

Glossary

clan   A family group. The Seminole have eight matrilineal clans—the bear, bigtown, bird, deer, otter, panther, snake, and wind.

chickee   A traditional, open-walled building with a thatched roof and raised floor. It was created by the Seminole for life in the Everglades.

cimarron   A Spanish word that means "runaway" or "wild."

commercial villages   Villages that were created to display Native American life for tourists.

conquer   To subdue another people through the use of force.

Corn Dance   An important ritual at the Green Corn Ceremony. It includes acts of purification and displays of manhood.

corporate charter   A document filed by founders of a corporation, describing its purpose, place of business, and other details about the corporation.

diaspora   The movement of people away from their original homelands.

Everglades   A subtropical ecosystem in southern Florida that is largely wetlands. It is now a national park.

Green Corn Ceremony   The most important celebration on the Seminole's traditional calendar. It is a celebration of the harvest and a festival of rebirth.

Indian Territory   The area west of the Mississippi River that was reserved for American Indians who were often removed from their homelands. It later became the state of Oklahoma.

kickbacks   Payments that are made in return for providing a job or other service.

matrilineal   A system of kinship in which family is traced only through the female line.

patchwork   A distinctive design on clothing that Seminole sew and wear.

Reconstruction   The era after the U.S. Civil War when the federal government tried to rebuild the war-torn South and provide freedom to former slaves.

removal   The process of forcing American Indians off of their homelands.

reservation   Lands that are held in trust by the federal government for use by an American Indian group.

subtropical wetlands   A hot and humid marsh that is suitable for varied wildlife.

sunbelt city   Newly formed cities in the southern and southwestern parts of the United States.

Termination   The policy after World War II to end the special relationship between American Indian groups and the federal government. It encouraged assimilation by putting Native American groups under state law and by ending the trust system that prevented their lands from being sold.

treaty   An agreement between nations or groups to resolve problems or establish rules for future behavior.

Bibliography

Bartram, William. *William Bartram on the Southeastern Indians.* Lincoln: University of Nebraska Press, 2002.

Bureau of Indian Affairs. Annual Narrative Report, Letter Group 75. Washington, D.C.: National Archives, 1933.

Cattelino, Jessica. *High Stakes: Florida Seminole Gaming and Sovereignty.* Durham, N.C.: Duke University Press, 2008.

Covington, James W. *The Seminole of Florida.* Gainesville: University Press of Florida, 1993.

Frank, Andrew K. *Creeks and Southerners: Biculturalism on the Early American Frontier.* Lincoln: University of Nebraska Press, 2005.

Jumper, Betty Mae and Patsy West. *A Seminole Legend: The Life of Betty Mae Tiger Jumper.* Gainesville: University Press of Florida, 2001.

Kersey, Harry A., Jr. *An Assumption of Sovereignty: Social and Political Transformation Among the Florida Seminole, 1953–1979.* Lincoln: University of Nebraska Press, 1996.

Kersey, Harry A., Jr. *The Seminole of Florida and the New Deal, 1933–1942.* Boca Raton: Florida Atlantic University Press, 1989.

Kersey, Harry A., Jr. *Pelts, Plumes and Hides: White Traders Among the Seminole Indians.* Boca Raton: Florida Atlantic University Press, 1980.

Kersey, Harry A. Jr. and Buffalo Tiger. *Buffalo Tiger: Life in the Everglades.* Lincoln: University of Nebraska Press, 2002.

MacCauley, Clay. *The Seminole Indians of Florida.* Washington, D.C.: Government Printing Office, 1887.

Mahon, John K. *History of the Second Seminole War, 1835–1842.* Gainesville: University of Florida Press, 1985.

McReynolds, Edwin C. The *Seminole.* Norman: University of Oklahoma Press, 1957.

Miller, Susan A. *Coacoochee's Bones: A Seminole Saga.* Lawrence: University Press of Kansas, 2003.

Nash, Roy. "Survey of the Seminole Indians of Florida." 71st Congress, 3rd Session, Senate Document 314. Washington, D.C.: Government Printing Office, 1931.

Porter, Kenneth Wiggins. *Black Seminole: The History of a Freedom-Seeking People.* Gainesville: University of Florida Press, 1996.

Romans, Bernard. *A Concise Natural History of East and West Florida* (1775). Victoria, Australia: Firebird Press, 1999.

Saunt, Claudio. *A New Order of Things: Power, Property and the Transformation of the Creek Indians.* New York: Cambridge University Press, 1999.

Sprague, John Titcomb. *The Origin, Progress, and Conclusions of the Florida War.* New York: D. Appleton and Co., 1848.

Sturtevant, William C. "Creek into Seminole." In *North American Indians in Historical Perspective,* edited by Eleanor B. Leacock and Nancy O. Lurie, 92–128. New York: Random House, 1971.

Sturtevant, William C. "R. H. Pratt's Report on the Seminole In 1879." *Florida Anthropologist* 9 (1956): 1–24.

Swanton, John R. *Early History of the Creek Indians and Their Neighbors.* Washington, D.C.: Government Printing Office, 1922.

"Termination of Federal Supervision over Certain Tribes of Indians. Joint Hearing before the Sub-Committee of the Committees on Interior and Insular Affairs." 83rd Congress, 1st session, on S 2747 and HR 7321, Part 8, Seminole Indians, Florida. Washington, D.C.: Government Printing Office, 1954.

Weisman, Brent R. *Like Beads on a String: A Culture History of the Seminole Indians in North Peninsular Florida.* Tuscaloosa: University of Alabama Press, 1989.

Weisman, Brent R. *Unconquered People: Florida's Seminole and Miccosukee Indians.* Gainesville: University Press of Florida, 1999.

West, Patsy. *The Enduring Seminole: From Alligator Wrestling to Ecotourism.* Gainesville: University Press of Florida, 1998.

Wickman, Patricia R. *Osceola's Legacy.* Tuscaloosa: University of Alabama Press, 1994.

Wright, J. Leitch, Jr. *Creeks and Seminole: Destruction and Regeneration of the Muscogulge People.* Lincoln: University of Nebraska Press, 1986.

Further Resources

Missall, John and Mary Lou Missall. *The Seminole Wars: America's Longest Indian Conflict*. Gainesville: University Press of Florida, 2004.

Mulroy, Kevin. *Freedom on the Border: The Seminole Maroons in Florida, the Indian Territory, Coahuila, and Texas*. Lubbock, Tex.: Texas Tech University Press, 2003.

———. *The Seminole Freedmen: A History*. Tulsa: University of Oklahoma Press, 2007.

Raffa, Edwina and Annelle Rigsby. *Escape to the Everglades*. Sarasota, Fla.: Pineapple Press, 2006.

Remini, Robert Vincent. *Andrew Jackson and His Indians Wars*. New York: Penguin, 2002.

Web Sites

Ah-Tah-Thi-Ki Tribal Museum
www.ahtahthiki.com
This is the official Web site of the Ah-Tah-Thi-Ki tribal museum for the Seminole Tribe of Florida. It has information about permanent and temporary exhibits as well as online exhiits.

Rebellion: John Horse and the Black Seminoles, the First Black Rebels to Beat American Slavery
www.johnhorse.com
This Web site explores the role of African Americans during the Second Seminole War. It contains many images and primary source documents.

Miccosukee Tribe of Indians of Florida
www.miccosukee.com
This is the official Web site of the Miccosukee Tribe. It contains information about contemporary Miccosukee life as well as about its history.

Museum of Florida History
www.museumoffloridahistory.com
This is the official Web site for the Museum of Florida History in Talla-hassee. It contains information and many images that reveal the history of Florida and the Seminole Tribe.

Seminole Tribe of Florida
www.seminoletribe.com
This is the official Web site of the Seminole Tribe of Florida. It has links to the Seminole Tribune *and other important information about the culture and history of the Seminole.*

Seminole Wars Foundation, Inc.
www.seminolewars.us
This is the Web site for the Seminole Wars Foundation, a nonprofit group that seeks to preserve Seminole War sites and educate the public about the wars.

Picture Credits

Index

About the Contributors

Author **ANDREW K. FRANK** is an associate professor of history at Florida State University. He teaches courses in the history of the Seminole Tribe and of Native Americans in general. He is the author of several books and articles on the Creek and Seminole, including *Creeks and Southerners: Biculturalism on the Early American Frontier* (Lincoln, 2005) and *The Routledge Historical Atlas of the American South* (New York, 1999).

Series editor **PAUL C. ROSIER** received his Ph.D. in American History from the University of Rochester in 1998. Dr. Rosier currently serves as associate professor of history at Villanova University (Villanova, Pennsylvania), where he teaches Native American History, American Environmental History, Global Environmental Justice Movements, History of American Capitalism, and World History.

In 2001, the University of Nebraska Press published his first book, *Rebirth of the Blackfeet Nation, 1912–1954;* in 2003, Greenwood Press published *Native American Issues* as part of its Contemporary Ethnic American Issues series. In 2006, he co-edited an international volume called *Echoes from the Poisoned Well: Global Memories of Environmental Injustice.* Dr. Rosier has also published articles in the *American Indian Culture and Research Journal,* the *Journal of American Ethnic History,* and the *Journal of American History.* His *Journal of American History* article, entitled "'They Are Ancestral Homelands: Race, Place, and Politics in Cold War Native America, 1945–1961,'" was selected for inclusion in *The Ten Best History Essays of 2006–2007,* published by Palgrave MacMillan in 2008; and it won the Western History Association's 2007 Arrell Gibson Award for Best Essay on the history of Native Americans. In 2009, Harvard University Press published his latest book, *Serving Their Country: American Indian Politics and Patriotism in the Twentieth Century.*